THE HISTORY OF THE RITE OF
HOLY WEEK
IN THE COPTIC ORTHODOX CHURCH

THE HISTORY OF THE RITE OF
HOLY WEEK
IN THE COPTIC ORTHODOX CHURCH

BY

DR. YOUHANNA NESSIM YOUSSEF

ST SHENOUDA PRESS
SYDNEY, AUSTRALIA
2023

THE HISTORY OF THE RITE OF HOLY WEEK
IN THE COPTIC ORTHODOX CHURCH
Dr Youhanna Nessim Youssef

COPYRIGHT © 2023
St. Shenouda Press

All rights reserved. Except for brief quotations in critical publications or reviews, no part of this book may be reproduced in any manner without prior written permission from the publisher.

ST SHENOUDA PRESS
8419 Putty Rd,
Putty, NSW, 2330
Sydney, Australia

www.stshenoudapress.com

ISBN 13: 978-0-6457703-0-8

All scripture quotations, unless otherwise indicated, are taken from the New King James Version®. Copyright © 1982 by Thomas Nelson, Inc. Used by permission. All rights reserved.

Contents

Acknowledgment 7

Introduction 9

CHAPTER IA 13
The Third Century

CHAPTER IB 15
The Fourth Century

CHAPTER II 33
The Fifth Century

CHAPTER III 49
The Sixth Century

CHAPTER IV 59
The Seventh—Eighth Century

CHAPTER V 61
The Ninth Century

CHAPTER VI 63
The Tenth Century

CHAPTER VII 65
The Eleventh Century

CHAPTER VIII 67
The Twelfth Century

CHAPTER IX 69
The Thirteenth- Fourteenth Century

CHAPTER X 79
The Fourteenth Century

CHAPTER XI — 95
The Fifteenth Century

CHAPTER XII — 107
The Seventeenth Century

CHAPTER XIII — 111
Textual Structure Of The Rite Of The Holy Week

CONCLUSION — 115

BIBLIOGRAPHY — 117

APPENDIX — 129

ACKNOWLEDGMENT

The author of this book would like to thank all who encouraged him to accomplish this work.

This book is an answer to many questions about the history of the Coptic Rite. The idea started during my study in Montpellier. Bishop Theophilus (Fr Ignatius al-Suriani) was the first to support this idea.

I had the privilege to attend the Holy Week in the Monastery of Moharraq, which enabled me to feel the depth of the Rite of the Coptic Church. On this occasion I would like to thank all the monks of that monastery. I would also like to express my gratitude to the monks of the monastery of al-Surian and especially H.G. Bishop Matteos who encouraged me to continue my research

Mr. Adel Athanasius, librarian of the Coptic Church in Melbourne, enabled this publication by providing me with many of the library's resources.

I am also indebted to the Libraries of the University of Melbourne, Monash University and to all my friends.

I was supported by the former director of Center for Early Christian Studies at the Australian Catholic University Pauline Allen, my colleagues in Saint Athanasius College- University of Divinity (Australia) and Eastern Christian Studies, University College Stockholm (Sweden)

Last but not least His Grace Bishop Suriel (former Bishop of Melbourne).

I would like to express my appreciation and gratitude to all those who are mentioned and to the many others whose support was invaluable to the actualization of this book

      To my wife and my daughters, I dedicate this book.

Youhanna Nessim Youssef

INTRODUCTION

Why this book?

In this book I tried to explore the Coptic rite of Holy Week. I found that the Coptic Rite is a compilation and an interaction of theological debates.

"The true story (of the Holy week) seems rather more complex... The Holy Week did not develop as a single integrated whole but as the result of the fusion of two previously distinct traditions"[1]

The books that examine the Coptic rite of Holy Week are very few. There are only two Arabic sources that tackle the topic at hand: a pamphlet which I published[2] in 1994 and a study by Fr Athanasius St Macarius.[3] Even then, these two approach the topic very differently. In the Byzantine Church however, there are many books relating to their traditions.[4]

---

1 Bradshaw, 1992, p.200-201.
2 Some remarks on the History and the development of the Rite of the Holy Week – Cairo 1997, 64p. (in Arabic)
3 Athanasius al-Maqari, The holy Pascha, the liturgical history and the rite of prayers In Arabic

Cairo 2010.×طقوس الصلوات/البصخة المقدسة، التاريخ الطقسي'اثناسيوس المقاري،

4 Such as A. Calivas, Great Week and Pascha in the Greek Orthodox Church. Brookline, MA: Holy Cross Orthodox Press1992. A. Schmemann, Holy Week: A Liturgical Explanation for the Days of Holy Week. Crestwood, NY: St. Vladimir's Seminary Press. 1961 H. Webrew, Orthodox Lent Holy Week and Easter: Liturgical Texts and Commentary. Crestwood, NY: St. Vladimir's Seminary Press 1997.

As I mentioned the Coptic liturgy is like a puzzle for which we do not possess all the pieces, therefore, I explored parallels in other Christian traditions.

My role, here, is like a geologist who studies the components and the layers of the Earth in order to know the composition of the soil, but it is not his role to change the environment and if he does so it will be considered as a threat to the ecology.

We ought to acknowledge that we are far from the theological caliber of those who contributed to the Coptic Rites such as Saint Severus of Antioch or Saint Peter the Fuller.

We have to highlight that the depth and spirituality of the hymns in the Coptic Rite of the Holy Week is far from what we actually hear as Arabic hymns.

The first chapter examines evidence from the first to the fourth centuries. The rite of the Holy Week as described by Egeria in the fourth century is compared to the contemporary practice of the Coptic Church. Further, the reader is provided with the History of the Trinitarian Doxology which is compared to the tunes of the hymn of glorifications, as well as a Syriac text. I conclude this chapter with the quotes from the Canons of Athanasius and some hints in the life of Pachomius.

In Chapter two, the Armenian lectionary of Jerusalem is studied as a crucial piece of evidence from the fifth century. It was concluded that this early witness inspired the Coptic Lectionary of the Holy Week.

In chapter three, I followed the evolution of five components of the Coptic rite in the sixth century, namely: the Trisagion, the Troparion ο μονογενης, the appendix of the troparion, the Troparia of the sext and none of Good Friday and finally the Wednesday of Job.

In the fourth chapter, the evolution of the rites behind prominent Holy Week hymns is found within resources from the seventh and eighth centuries. This includes the Greek hymn of Judas, the Good Friday hymn of the Thief and the hymn of ⲫⲁⲓ ⲉⲧⲁϥⲉⲛϥ .

In the fifth chapter the Georgian lectionary of Jerusalem and the Coptic Sahidic lectionary were studied.

INTRODUCTION 11

In the sixth chapter, the tenth century is explored, and the prayer of the foot washing is unearthed

In the seventh chapter, the Canons of Pope Christodulos (1047-1077AD) are reviewed.

In chapter eight, the 12th century writing of Abû al-Makârim is delved into.

In the ninth chapter, the lectionary and the Turuhât are probed- which are assumed to have taken their final form in the thirteenth and fourteenth centuries.

The tenth chapter deals with two Copto-Arabic writers i.e. Ibn Kabar and Ibn Saba' of the fourteenth century.

The eleventh chapter is a study of the litany of the evening, the canon of Good Friday and the work of two Muslim authors Maqrizi and Qalqašandi of the fifteenth century.

The twelfth chapter is the textual structure of the rite of Holy Week.

I add as an appendix, a letter of Gregory of Nyssa against the pilgrimage in Jerusalem.

In this edition, the original texts are literally translated and I put between brackets the transliteration and the translation.

Ultimately, this book will demonstrate that the Coptic rite of the Holy Week is mainly derived from the rite of Jerusalem. Moreover, certain prominent hymns were added, or contributed to by a sister Church, to satisfy theological needs or for explanation of readings.

This work aims to inspire the readers to continue building on this preliminary foundation in order to fill the gap in research.

CHAPTER IA
THE THIRD CENTURY

In the third century, Christianity was in its infancy, one of the first text we possess about the Pascha is the text attributed to Melito of Sardis.

His text on Pascha may be considered as the first and the most widespread in Christianity as it survived in most languages of the early Christianity such as Greek, Latin, Coptic and Syriac.[5] Melito of Sardis made a commentary on Exodus 12 and gave some hints about the practice of the pascha.[6] In this context, it developed as a polemical reaction to the pagan mysteries practiced in Asia Minor.

There are also two other texts relating to the Holy Week from the third century, the first is attributed to Pseudo-Hippolytus (c. 170c.-236AD) who was a presbyter and probably a schismatic bishop of Rome. He wrote numerous works in Greek on theological and ecclesiastical subjects. Some of their titles are listed on the base of an early statue of him, found in Rome in 1551, now in the Vatican Library. Two of the most important are *Philosophoumena*, written against Gnosticism and other heresies, and the *Apostolic Tradition*, one of the most helpful sources for the student of early canon law, liturgy, and church customs. Hippolytus is a saint in the Orthodox and Roman Catholic churches but not in the Coptic church.[7]

---

5   Geerard, 1983, §1092, pp36-38.
6   Drago, " (2008, pp. 27-47.
7   Segelberg, 1991, p. 1235-1236.

The other text is the Apocryphal Epistles of the Apostles which survives in Coptic fragments and complete Ethiopic and Latin versions, where the Eucharist is called *Pascha* and regarded as a memorial of the death of Jesus:

> But do you commemorate my death. Now, when the *Pascha* comes, one of you shall be cast into prison for My name's sake

This indicates that the celebration of the Pascha was known in the second century.[8]

---

8   Quasten, volum 1, 1966, p, 151-153.

CHAPTER IB

THE FOURTH CENTURY

The Rite Of The Holy Week In The Fourth Century According To Egeria

Egeria was a French Lady (we are not sure whether she was an abbess or from a noble Family) who made the pilgrimage to the Middle East (Egypt, Palestine, and Edessa) between 381-384 A.D. She left a detailed description of the Rite of the Holy Week in Jerusalem.[9]

We will see that the actual Coptic Rite has the same structure as the Rite of Jerusalem in the Fourth Century (our comment will be put between brackets and with bold characters).

Holy Week And The Festivals Of Easter[10]

Saturday before Palm Sunday - Station at Bethany

Now when the seventh week has come, that is, when two weeks, including the seventh, are left before Easter, everything is done on each day as in the weeks that, are past, except that the vigils of the sixth weekday, which were kept in the

---

9 cf Egérie, 1982, p. 271-293. Her name for a while was considered as Etheria = Heavenly but the studies of Professor Maraval showed clearly that her name was Egeria a proper name from Greek Mythology.

10 The English text is taken from the translation prepared by John Abela ofm based on articles and research by Virgilio Corbo ofm, Michele Piccirillo ofm and Eugenio Alliata ofm http://www.christusrex.org/www1/jhs/TSeger04.html#Target15

Anastasis during the first six weeks, are, in the seventh week, kept in Sion, and with the same customs that obtained during the six weeks in the Anastasis. For throughout the whole vigil psalms and antiphons are said appropriate both to the place and to the day.

And when the morning of the Sabbath begins to dawn, the bishop offers the oblation. And at the dismissal the archdeacon lifts his voice and says: "Let us all be ready to-day at the seventh hour in the Lazarium." And so, as the seventh hour approaches, all go to the Lazarium, that is, Bethany, situated at about the second milestone from the city.

And as they go from Jerusalem to the Lazarium, there is, about five hundred paces from the latter place, a church in the street on that spot where Mary the sister of Lazarus met with the Lord. Here, when the bishop arrives, all the monks meet him, and the people enter the church, and one hymn and one antiphon are said, and that passage is read in the Gospel where the sister of Lazarus meets the Lord. Then, after prayer has been made, and when all have been blessed, they go thence with hymns to the Lazarium.

And on arriving at the Lazarium, so great a multitude assembles that not only the place itself, but also the fields around, are full of people. Hymns and antiphons suitable to the day and to the place are said, and likewise all the lessons are read. Then, before the dismissal, notice is given of Easter, that is, the priest ascends to a higher place and reads the passage that is written in the Gospel: When Jesus six days before the Passover had come to Bethany, and the rest. So, that passage having been read and notice given of Easter, the dismissal is made.

This is done on that day because, as it is written in the Gospel, these events took place in Bethany six days before the Passover; there being six days from the Sabbath to the fifth weekday on which, after supper, the Lord was taken by night. Then all return to the city direct to the Anastasis, and lucernare[11] takes place according to custom.

(The Coptic Church till now has special hymn for Lazarus Saturday. The Text of Egeria shows that this tradition is very ancient).

Palm Sunday: Services in the Churches.

> On the next day, that is, the Lord's Day, which begins the Paschal week, and which they call here the Great Week, when all the customary services from cockcrow until morning have taken place in the *Anastasis* and at the *Cross*, they proceed on the morning of the Lord's Day according to custom to the greater church, which is called the *martyrium*. It is called the *martyrium* because it is in Golgotha behind the Cross, where the Lord suffered.
>
> When all that is customary has been observed in the great church, and before the dismissal is made, the archdeacon lifts his voice and says first: "Throughout the whole week, beginning from to-morrow, let us all assemble in the *martyrium*, that is, in the great church, at the ninth hour." Then he lifts his voice again, saying: "Let us all be ready to-day in Eleona at the seventh hour."
>
> So when the dismissal has been made in the great church! that is, the *martyrium*, the bishop is escorted with hymns to the *Anastasis*, and after all things that are customary on the Lord's Day have been done there, after the dismissal from the *martyrium*, every one hastens home to eat, that all may be ready at the beginning of the seventh hour in the church in Eleona, on the Mount of Olives, where is the cave in which the Lord was wont to teach.

Procession[12] with Palms on the Mount of Olives.

> Accordingly at the seventh hour all the people go up to the Mount of Olives, that is, to Eleona, and the bishop with them,

---

11   Lucernare means vigil, from the Latin word Lucerna (=lamp).
12   It is noteworthy that the procession of the Resurrection and Palm Sunday have been established in order to make people participate in the Economy of

to the church, where hymns and antiphons suitable to the day and to the place are said, and lessons in like manner. And when the ninth hour approaches, they go up with hymns to the Imbomon, that is, to the place whence the Lord ascended into heaven, and there they sit down, for all the people are always bidden to sit when the bishop is present; the deacons alone always stand. Hymns and antiphons suitable to the day and to the place are said, interspersed with lections and prayers.

And as the eleventh hour approaches, the passage from the Gospel is read, where the children, carrying branches and palms, met the Lord, saying; Blessed is He that cometh in the name of the Lord, and the bishop immediately rises, and all the people with him, and they all go on foot from the top of the Mount of Olives, all the people going before him with hymns and antiphons, answering one to another: Blessed is He that cometh in the name of the Lord.

And all the children in the neighborhood, even those who are too young to walk, are carried by their parents on their shoulders, all of them bearing branches, some of palms and some of olives, and thus the bishop is escorted in the same manner as the Lord was of old.

For all, even those of rank, both matrons and men, accompany the bishop all the way on foot in this manner, making these responses, from the top of the mount to the city, and thence through the whole city to the Anastasis, going very slowly lest the people should be wearied; and thus, they arrive at the *Anastasis* at a late hour. And on arriving, although it is late, lucernare takes place, with prayer at the Cross; after which the people are dismissed.

Salvation such as the Entry of Jesus to Jerusalem, or the way from death to life which Jesus Christ had paved for us. This rite is one of the most ancient rites in the Church known since the IV century. The other processions such as the last hour of the Holy Friday or the procession of a Bishop is a cortege and people do not participate cf. Corbon, 1996, p. 341-359 especially p 345.

CHAPTER IB: *The Fourth Century*

(Actually, one of the characteristic features of the Palm Sunday is the procession of the Holy Cross in the Church. I will discuss the development of this rite later)

Monday in Holy Week

> On the next day, the second weekday, everything that is customary is done from the first cockcrow until morning in the *Anastasis*; also, at the **third** and **sixth** hours everything is done that is customary throughout the whole of Quadragesima. but at the **ninth** hour all assemble in the great church, that is the *martyrium*, where hymns and **antiphons** are said continuously until the first hour of the night and lessons suitable to the day and the place are read, interspersed always with prayers.

> Lucernare takes place when its hour approaches, that is, so that it is already night when the dismissal at the *martyrium* is made. When the dismissal has been made, the bishop is escorted thence with hymns to the *Anastasis*, where, when he has entered, one hymn is said, followed by a prayer; the catechumens and then the faithful are blessed, and the dismissal is made.

(It is quite clear that the actual Coptic rite of the Holy Week has its roots from the rite of Jerusalem in early Christianity. We can easily recognize the structure of hours as in the Coptic Rite. In this text, the morning, third (tierce), sixth (sext), ninth (none) hour prayers are clearly mentioned.

In addition to that, we have the way of singing i.e. antiphons - singing with two choir alternatively - which is actually observed for the Coptic hymns of ⲡⲟⲩⲣⲟ ⲛⲧⲉ ϯϩⲓⲣⲏⲛⲏ *"O king of Peace" or* ⲑⲱⲕ ⲧⲉ ϯϫⲟⲙ *"To you is the power")*

Tuesday in Holy Week

> On the third weekday everything is done as on the second, with this one thing added--that late at night, after the dismissal of the *martyrium*, and after the going to the *Anastasis* and

after the dismissal there, all proceed at that hour by night to the church, which is on the mount Eleona.

And when they have arrived at that church, the bishop enters the cave where the Lord was wont to teach His disciples, and after receiving the book of the Gospel, he stands and himself reads the words of the Lord which are written in the Gospel according to Matthew, where He says: Take heed that no man deceives you. And the bishop reads through the whole of that discourse, and when he has read it, prayer is made, the catechumens and the faithful are blessed, the dismissal is made, and everyone returns from the mount to his house, it being already very late at night.

Wednesday in Holy Week.

On the fourth weekday everything is done as on the second and third weekdays throughout the whole day from the first cockcrow onwards, but after the dismissal has taken place at the Martyrium by night, and the bishop has been escorted with hymns to the Anastasis, he at once enters the cave which is in the Anastasis, and stands within the rails; but the priest stands before the rails and receives the Gospel, and reads the passage where Judas Iscariot went to the Jews and stated what they should give him that he should betray the Lord. And when the passage has been read, there is such a moaning and groaning of all the people that no one can help being moved to tears at that hour. Afterwards prayer follows, then the blessing, first of the catechumens, and then of the faithful, and the dismissal is made.

(*We may notice here that the Monday, Tuesday and Wednesday have the same rite. The reading of the Wednesday is the passage of Judas which is observed in the Coptic Church*)

Maundy Thursday: Mass celebrated twice.

On the fifth weekday everything that is customary is done from the first cockcrow until morning at the *Anastasis*, and also at the third and at the sixth hours. But at the eighth hour all the people gather together at the *martyrium* according to custom, only earlier than on other days, because the dismissal must be made sooner. Then, when the people are gathered together, all that should be done is done, and the oblation is made on that day at the *martyrium*, the dismissal taking place about the tenth hour. But before the dismissal is made there, the archdeacon raises his voice and says: "Let us all assemble at the first hour of the night in the church which is in Eleona, for great toil awaits us to-day, in this very night."

Then, after the dismissal at the martyrium, they arrive behind the Cross, where only one hymn is said and prayer is made, and the bishop offers the oblation there, and all communicate. Nor is the oblation ever offered behind the Cross on any day throughout the year, except on this one day. And after the dismissal there they go to the Anastasis, where prayer is made, the catechumens and the faithful are blessed according to custom, and the dismissal is made.

Night Station on the Mount of Olives.

And so, everyone hastens back to his house to eat, because immediately after they have eaten, all go to Eleona to the church wherein is the cave where the Lord was with His Apostles on this very day.

There then, until about the fifth hour of the night, hymns, and antiphons suitable to the day and to the place are said, lessons, too, are read in like manner, with prayers interspersed, and the passages from the Gospel are read where the Lord addressed His disciples on that same day as He sat in the same cave which is in that church.

And they go thence at about the sixth hour of the night with hymns up to the Imbomon, the place whence the Lord ascended into heaven, where again lessons are read, hymns and antiphons suitable to the day are said, and all the prayers which are made by the bishop are also suitable both to the day and to the place.

Stations at Gethsemane.

> And at the first cockcrow they come down from the Imbomon with hymns, and arrive at the place where the Lord prayed, as it is written in the Gospel: and He was withdrawn (from them) about a stone's cast, and prayed, and the rest. There is in that place a graceful church The bishop and all the people enter, a prayer suitable to the place and to the day is said, with one suitable hymn, and the passage from the Gospel is read where He said to His disciples: Watch, that ye enter not into temptation; the whole passage is read through, and prayer is made.
>
> And then all, even to the smallest child, go down with the Bishop, on foot, with hymns to Gethsemane; where, on account of the great number of people in the crowd, who are wearied owing to the vigils and weak through the daily fasts, and because they have so great a hill to descend, they come very slowly with hymns to Gethsemane. And over two hundred church candles are made ready to give light to all the people.
>
> On their arrival at Gethsemane, first a suitable prayer is made, then a hymn is said, then the passage of the Gospel is read where the Lord was taken. And when this passage has been read there is so great a moaning and groaning of all the people, together with weeping, that their lamentation may be heard perhaps as far as the city.

Return to Jerusalem.

> From that hour they go with hymns to the city on foot, reaching the gate about the time when one man begins to be able to recognise another, and thence right on through the midst of the city; all, to a man, both great and small, rich and poor, all are ready there, for on that special day not a soul withdraws from the vigils until morning. Thus, the bishop is escorted from Gethsemane to the gate, and thence through the whole of the city to the Cross.

(We may notice that the prayer of matins, tierce and none are done earlier than usual because there is the prayer of Basin and the Mass. The Night of Good Friday corresponds to the stations at Gethsemane, but it is done through readings instead of going to the place)

Good Friday: Service at Daybreak.

And when they arrive before the *Cross* the daylight is already growing bright. There the passage from the Gospel is read where the Lord is brought before Pilate, with everything that is written concerning that which Pilate spoke to the Lord or to the Jews; the whole is read. And afterwards the bishop addresses the people, comforting them for that they have toiled all night and are about to toil during that same day, (bidding) them not be weary, but to have hope in God, Who will for that toil give them a greater reward. And encouraging them as he is able, he addresses them thus: "Go now, each one of you, to your houses, and sit down awhile, and all of you be ready here just before the second hour of the day, that from that hour to the sixth you may be able to behold the holy wood of the Cross, each one of us believing that it will be profitable to his salvation; then from the sixth hour we must all assemble again in this place, that is, before the Cross, that we may apply ourselves to lections and to prayers until night."

The Column of the Flagellation

After this, when the dismissal at the *Cross* has been made, that is, before the sun rises, they all go at once with fervor to Sion, to pray at the column at which the Lord was scourged. And returning thence they sit for awhile in their houses, and presently all are ready.

Veneration of the Cross.

Then a chair is placed for the bishop in Golgotha behind the Cross, which is now standing; the bishop duly takes his seat in the chair, and a table covered with a linen cloth is placed before him; the deacons stand round the table, and a silver-gilt casket is brought in which is the holy wood of the Cross. The casket is opened and (the wood) is taken out, and both the wood of the Cross and the title are placed upon the table.

Now, when it has been put upon the table, the bishop, as he sits, holds the extremities of the sacred wood firmly in his hands, while the deacons who stand around guard it. It is guarded thus because the custom is that the people, both faithful and catechumens, come one by one and, bowing down at the table, kiss the sacred wood and pass through. And because, I know not when, someone is said to have bitten off and stolen a portion of the sacred wood, it is thus guarded by the deacons who stand around, lest anyone approaching should venture to do so again.

And as all the people pass by one by one, all bowing themselves, they touch the Cross and the title, first with their foreheads and then with their eyes; then they kiss the Cross and pass through, but none lays his hand upon it to touch it. When they have kissed the Cross and have passed through, a deacon stands holding the ring of Solomon and the horn from which the kings were anointed; they kiss the horn also and gaze at the ring... all the people are passing through up to the sixth hour, entering by one door and going out by another; for this is done in the same place where, on the preceding day, that is, on the fifth weekday, the oblation was offered.

Station before the Cross. The Three Hours.

And when the sixth hour has come, they go before the Cross, whether it be in rain or in heat, the place being open to the air, as it were, a court of great size and of some beauty between the Cross and the *Anastasis*; here all the people assemble in such great numbers that there is no thoroughfare. The chair is placed for the bishop before the Cross, and from the sixth to the ninth hour nothing else is done, but the reading of lessons, which are read thus: first from the psalms wherever the Passion is spoken of, then from the Apostle, either from the epistles of the Apostles or from their Acts, wherever they have spoken of the Lord's Passion; then the passages from the Gospels, where He suffered, are read. Then the readings from the prophets where they foretold that the Lord should suffer, then from the Gospels where He mentions His Passion.

Thus, from the sixth to the ninth hours the lessons are so read, and the hymns said, that it may be shown to all the people that whatsoever the prophets foretold of the Lord's Passion is proved from the Gospels and from the writings of the Apostles to have been fulfilled. And so, through all those three hours the people are taught that nothing was done which had not been foretold, and that nothing was foretold which was not wholly fulfilled. Prayers also suitable to the day are interspersed throughout.

The emotion shown and the mourning by all the people at every lesson and prayer is wonderful; for there is none, either great or small, who, on that day during those three hours, does not lament more than can be conceived, that the Lord had suffered those things for us. Afterwards, at the beginning of the ninth hour, there is read that passage from the Gospel according to John where He gave up the ghost. This read, prayer and the dismissal follow.

(We notice here that also for the sext and none the current readings are also from the Apostle Paul ⲉⲑⲃⲉ ϯⲁⲛⲁⲥⲧⲁⲥⲓⲥ *(ethve ti-anastasis)* and ϯⲉⲡⲓⲥⲧⲟⲗⲏ *(ti-epistoli)* in addition to many hymns which will be discussed later in this book)

Evening Offices

And when the dismissal before the Cross has been made, all things are done in the greater church, at the martyrium, which are customary during this week from the ninth hour --when the assembly takes place in the martyrium--until late. And after the dismissal at the *martyrium*, they go to the *Anastasis*, where, when they arrive, the passage from the Gospel is read where Joseph begged the Body of the Lord from Pilate and laid it in a new sepulcher. And this reading ended, a prayer is said, the catechumens are blessed, and the dismissal is made. But on that day no announcement is made of a vigil at the *Anastasis*, because it is known that the people are tired; nevertheless, it is the custom to watch there. So all of the people who are willing, or rather, who are able, keep watch, and they who are unable do not watch there until the morning. Those of the clergy, however, who are strong or young keep vigil there, and hymns and antiphons are said throughout the whole night until morning; a very great crowd also keep night-long watch, some from the late hour and some from midnight, as they

(This office corresponds to the actual Rite of Apocalypse (*Abughalamisis/Apokalypsis* ⲁⲡⲟⲕⲁⲗⲩⲯⲓⲥ))

Vigil of Easter

Now, on the next day, the Sabbath, everything that is customary is done at the third hour and also at the sixth; the service at the ninth hour, however, is not held on the Sabbath, but the Paschal vigils are prepared in the great church, the *martyrium*. The Paschal vigils are kept as with us, with this one addition, that the children when they have been baptised and clothed, and when they issue from the font, are led with the bishop first to the *Anastasis*.

The bishop enters the rails of the *Anastasis*, and one hymn is said, then the bishop says a prayer for them, and then he goes with them to the greater church, where, according to custom, all the people are keeping watch. Everything is done there that is customary with us also, and after the oblation has been made, the dismissal takes place. After the dismissal of the vigils has been made in the greater church, they go at once with hymns to the *Anastasis*, where the passage from the Gospel about the Resurrection is read. Prayer is made, and the bishop again makes the oblation. But everything is done quickly on account of the people, that they should not be delayed any longer, and so the people are dismissed. The dismissal of the vigils takes place on that day at the same hour as with us.

Doxology To The Holy Trinity

ⲆⲞⲜⲀ ⲠⲀⲦⲢⲒ ⲔⲈ ⲨⲒⲰ ⲔⲈ ⲀⲅⲒⲰ ⲠⲚⲈⲨⲘⲀⲦⲒ
"Glory to the Father the Son and the Holy Spirit"
According to Philostorgius the Historian[13], in circa 350, the Nicene opponents of Leontius of Antioch had composed a doxology "Glory be to the Father and to the Son and to the Holy Spirit", implying that both Son and the Holy Spirit were consubstantial with the Father. This was different to the traditional Antiochene version, 'Glory to the Father through the Son and in the Holy Spirit', which, seemed to imply a subordination of the latter two persons to the Father.[14]

ⲔⲀⲒ ⲨⲠⲈⲢ ⲦⲞⲨ

"In order to make us worthy to hear the Holy Gospel, we beseech our Lord and our God. Let us listen to the Holy Gospel, in wisdom."
One of the most ancient mentions about the history of hymns during Good Friday, is a Syriac Manuscript preserved in the British Library, and dated to 411 A.D. (This manuscript is a translation of a lost Greek original which goes back to the year 362 A.D., and belongs to the Church of Nicomedia where Egypt and Alexandria are mentioned 19 times in 4 folios.)

We find "The Good Friday after the Passover, a remembrance of the Martyrs is done"[15]

This remark can explain the resemblance between the hymn of Glorification of the Saints ⲀⲠⲈⲔⲢⲀⲚ (a pekran) and the introduction to the Coptic Gospel ⲔⲀⲒ ⲨⲠⲈⲢ ⲦⲞⲨ (Kai yper tou). We may think that the remembrance of the Martyrs in Early Christianity was with the remembrance of the Suffering of Christ. It is probable that these hymns were once one hymn.

---

13   Philostorgius, was a resident of Constantinople, who completed his Church History (Twelve books),at around 425 A.D.. They are mainly preserved in extracts of Photius. He gave particular attention to secular history and strongly emphasized the Arian standpoint cf. Altaner, 1960, p.274.
14   J. Bidez, Philostorgius . Kirchengeschichte, GCS 21, Leipzig 1913, III.13 mentioned by W.H.C. Frend, 1979, p. 167-168.
Philostragius born in 318 in Cappadocia.
15   Nau, 1912, p. 15.

The words of the hymn ⲁ ⲡⲉⲕⲣⲁⲛ were composed by Bishop Michael al-Maʿargi in the fourteenth century for the commemoration of saint Barsuma the Naked[16] (not saint Antony)[17], however the tune is ancient.

The Canons Of Athanasius

These canons were written around 370 AD. They are preserved in Coptic fragments and in Arabic. We find in the §§ 57-60 of these canons some arrangements concerning the Holy Week:-

> §57 In the week of the holy Pascha (all the priest shall sleep in the church).[18] *They shall gather all of them together on Friday, at the **third hour**; for this is the h*our wherein they did set about the crucifixion of our Saviour. If any be not present, he shall suffer reproof. And if he be an husbandman in the field, he shall not delay until the six hour. The deacons shall separate themselves into two parts among the people, helping one another, giving heed unto quietness among the people at the doors. Weeping children and such as talk among instruction, or him that behaveth himself deliberately without instruction, or him that behaveth himself unseemly shall they put forth. The doorkeepers shall keep watch at the outer doors and shall not suffer any of the scoffers nor any they have put forth to enter ere they be bidden. Likewise, the deacons shall stand at the second door. In case there be a press at the outer door, then shall they help the doorkeepers or if the deacons have need of doorkeepers to help them in keeping of order among the people, then shall these help them. All this let them do that the word of God may be glorified and the people hear in quietness and that silence be in the whole church, until they finish the word of God with the blessing. But if any of them talk with a loud voice, the blame falleth upon the presbyter, for that the deacons have not trained the people. During the Pascha the priests shall fast two days together. But

---

16   Maged Sobhi Rizk, 2008, p. 193-212..
17   As it is known that Saint Antony ordered his disciple to hide his body and no tomb of this saint is identified till now, while the hymn is talking about the tomb full of blessing and the blessed body.
18   Not in the Coptic fragments

the readers shall eat everyday, nor shall they do aught save what all the people do in their eating, as it is said, 'Eat ye the bread in affliction', that is to say, bread wherein no sweetness and herbs wherein no sweetness is.

§58 The readers shall understand what they say and them that would learn shall they instruct and teach without grudging but rather the more with gladness, because that those do ask what is good.

§59 The singers shall sing nought but the book of Psalms and likewise teach others without grudging to sing, that God may make His dwelling in the whole people, from the head to the foot.

§60 No priest shall tarry behind from the eight hour of the day onward, and they shall be gathered together, until the time of the appearing of the stars in heaven at evening. They shall read ere they let the people depart, they praying, and hearing the lessons, that they may be worthy of the Pascha in joy and gladness. And as for those things which they do at the Pascha, they shall eat and drink in wisdom, without drunkenness.[19]

From what we read, we can conclude that there were long prayers based essentially on psalms and readings. The churches were so crowded, and the task of the deacons was very difficult.

The Passover During The Time Of Saint Pachomius

Pachomius, the founder of cenobitic monasticism, established a monastery at Tabennisi in Thebaid c. 320 A.D. He wrote the first monastic rule in Coptic (d.346 A.D.)

His life and his writings inform us about the Holy Week during his time in Upper Egypt. It is one of the rare Coptic sources on this subject.

St. Theodore disciple of St. Pachomius used to assemble with brethren during the days of the Passover.[20]

---

19 Riedel and Crum, 1904, p. 38-40, 125-126.
20 Veilleux, 1980, p. 205.

> "This is how our father Theodore used to attend to their strengthening by means of the word and perfect teaching of the righteous man, our father Pachomius. While they celebrated the holy Passover of the Lord, he would dispose of all their affairs according to the traditions of our father Pachomius and they would celebrate the holy Resurrection of our Lord Jesus Christ. Then he would pray over them all and dismiss them in peace after having transferred many of them from one community to another for sake of their salvation."[21]

St. Pachomius used to give his instructions for the brethren on the six days of the Passover, we have chosen this paragraph as a sample of the instructions

> "Let us not lose heart at all during these holy days, but let the one who gives himself to fasting with joy, silence, wisdom, and great tranquility, who keeps himself pure from a variety of foods, who keeps from idle pleasures, who practices genuflections and incessant prayers, who is given to lack of sleep and frequent watches, in short, let everyone watch over his steadfastness, so that what is written in Acts will happen to us, Some on planks, some on gear of the ship and thus all came safe to the shore.[22]

Saint Pachomius and his disciple Theodore used to send a letter to the monasteries calling all brethren to assemble in the great monastery called Phbow in the days of the Passover and to share all together in the same celebration.[23]

We possess a letter from Theophilus (385-412 AD) to Horsiesios abbot of the monastery of Pachomius in Upper Egypt.[24] This letter came to our knowledge from the manuscripts of Strasbourg and some papyrus found in Fayoum.

In this letter, we find the rite of Baptism during the Great Week. The baptismal font would be covered with a veil. The feast of Resurrection

---

21   Ibid., p243.
22   Veilleux, 1982, p. 48.
23   Ibid., p. 63-67, 123-125.
24   Crum and Ehrhard, 1915, p 12-5, Orlandi 1990, p. 109-126.

was a double feast- Baptism of the new convert and Resurrection. After the celebration the archbishop invited Horsiesios for a banquet.

This rite is now celebrated on the sixth Sunday of the Lent in order to allow the neophyte to attend Passion Week.

CHAPTER II
THE FIFTH CENTURY

Hymn Of The Maundy Thursday

> "In Your mystical Supper, today, make me a participant.
> I will not reveal Your mystery to Your enemies.
> I will not kiss falsely like Judas
> But like the Thief, I believe and confess to You:
> Remember-me O Lord when You come in Your kingdom."

This hymn is included in the book of the Holy Week (the edition of Attalah Arsenius al-Muharraqi p.154) as one of the hymns of the "Alexandrians"

This hymn is found in Constantinople in the sixth century by Byzantine Chronicles, and before this date in a Georgian translation made in Palestine.[25] It was introduced to the Byzantine liturgy of Saint Basil for the Maundy Thursday in the sixth century.[26] Some scholars think that this hymn was directed against some heretics, perhaps Gnostics?

By using the word "today" in this hymn, the member of the Church asks to personally partake in the last Supper that took place 2000 years ago.

---

25 Renoux, 2010, p. 81-91.
26 Taft, 1978, p. 54-76.

The faithful is invited to partake in this act that has special power for the salvation of mankind, as "an actualization of the event celebrated".[27]

The Armenian Lectionary Of Jerusalem As A Witness Of The Liturgy Of Jerusalem [28]

Since the beginning of the twentieth century, specialists attracted the attention of the importance of the rites of Jerusalem for the formation and evolution of the liturgies of the East and the West.

Our first witness, as mentioned before, is the description of Egeria.[29] The second document is the Armenian lectionary of Jerusalem. This document is a translation of a lost Greek text. It contains two of the most ancient manuscripts known, Jerusalem 121 and Paris 44, which refer to a tradition in the beginning of the fifth century.[30] Below are select readings from the Palm Sunday till Good Friday.

The Lectionary for the Palm Sunday

> Let us assemble in the holy Martyrium: in the city and let us sing this canon: (Ps. 97 [98]: 8-9.) "Let the hills be joyful together before the Lord for he comes to judge"

> A reading from the Epistle of Paul the Apostle to the Ephesians (Ephes. 1: 3-10)

> Alleluia Ps 96 [97]
> "The Lord has reigns let the earth rejoice…"

> Gospel according to Matthew 20: 29- 21:17
> "And as they departed from Jericho… And He left them and went out the city into Bethany and lodged there."[31]

---

27   Lossky, 2011, p. 283-295.
28   For the introduction see Renoux, 1969, p.1-215.
29   See chapter 1.
30   Renoux, 1971, p. 144-289.
31   The Ms Paris 44 the reading stops in verse 11 "And the multitude said this is Jesus the prophet of Nazareth of Galilee"

On the same day at the ninth hour, we ascend to the Mount of Olives with branches of palms where we chant and pray.

At the eleventh hour we descend to the Holy Anastasis, and we sing psalm 117 [118][26] "Blessed be He who comes in the name of the Lord."

The Coptic rite does not use the Ps 97 however the meaning is reflected in the Tarh (exposition) of the Palm Sunday "Rise to the high mountains…"

We find the procession of the Mount of Olives which became in the Coptic rite as the procession of the Palm Sunday.

We may notice that the service ended in the ninth hour as in our liturgical rite today, we read the ninth hour just after the Eucharist.

The Eleventh hour is celebrated in the Anastasis as in our rite today in the afternoon.

The lectionary for the Monday

Monday for the fast of Pascha, let us assemble in the holy Martyrium in the city at the tenth hours.

Reading of the Genesis: (Gen. 1: 1- 3) "In the beginning God…and He placed at the East of the Garden of Eden Cherubim and a flaming sword which turned everyway, to keep the way of the tree of life.

The second reading from Proverbs: (Proverbs 1:2-9)

"To know wisdom and instruction….in order that your head receives crown and chains about your neck."

The third reading:(Is 40:1-8)

"Comfort, comfort My people… and the word of the Lord remains eternally.

Response (Ps. 64[65])

"Listen to us, God our Saviour, the hope of all the ends of the earth.

Gospel Matthew 20:17-28

"And Jesus was going out of Jerusalem… Just as the Son of Man did not come to be served but to serve and to give His Life a ransom for many."

The first reading is still observed in the first hour of the Monday of the Holy Pascha
The second and the third readings and the psalm are read in the ninth hour of the Monday of the Holy Pascha.
The Gospel of Matthew is read in the ninth hour of Palm Sunday and the eleventh hour of Palm Sunday.

The Lectionary for the Tuesday

On Tuesday let us assemble in the mount of the Olives at the tenth hour and we read this canon

First reading (Gen 6: 9- 9:17)

"This is genealogy of Noah… And this is the sign of the covenant which I have establish between Me and you and all flesh that is up the earth"

The second reading from Proverbs:(Pr. 9:1-11)

"Wisdom has built her house… And you will live long time and years will be added to you."

CHAPTER II: *The Fifth Century*

The third reading:(Is 40: 9:17)

"Get up in the high mountain…and all nations before Him are as nothing and they are counted by Him less than nothing."

Response: Ps 24[25]:1-2

"To You, O Lord, I lift my soul , O my God, I trust in You let me not be ashamed forever."

Gospel of Matthew: (Mat 24:3- 26: 2)

"Now as He sat on the Mount of the Olives… You know that after two days is the Passover and the Son of Man will be delivered up to be crucified."

All the readings are still observed in the ninth hour of the Tuesday of the Holy Pascha, except part of the Gospel is read in the ninth hour and continued in the Eleventh hour.

The lectionary for the Wednesday

On Wednesday at the tenth hour, let us assemble in the Saint martyrium in the city and let us read this canon.[32]

(Gen. 18:1-19:30)

"And the Lord appeared to him in the plains of Mamre… and he dwelt in a cave he and his two daughters"

The second reading: (Pr. 1:10-19)

"My son, if the sinners entices you do not consent… So are the ways of everyone who is greedy for gain. It takes away the life of its owners."

---

32   The texts of this canon treat the sin.

The third reading: (Zak 11: 11-14)

"And the Cananeans of my flock knew that his was the word of the Lord… Then I cut in two my staff. Bonds, that I might break the brotherhood between Judah and Israel."

Psalm Response:(Ps.40 [41] 5)

"I said: "Lord, have mercy upon me and heal my soul for I sin."

Then after reading the psalm let us descend to the Holy Anastasis and we read the Gospel of Matthew:

The Gospel: (Mat. 26: 3-16)

"Then the chief Priests and the scribes and the elders of the people assembled … So from that time he sought opportunity to betray him

The first reading is replaced in the Coptic rite by the reading of Genesis 24: 1-9.

The second reading is the same.

The third reading is read on the ninth hour of Wednesday and in the first hour of the Good Friday.

The psalm and the Gospel are still used for the ninth hour for the Holy Wednesday.

The lectionary for the Thursday

The Thursday of the Old Covenant, about which Jesus said to his to his disciples "I would like to partake the Passover with you." Let us assemble from the seventh hour in the Holy Martyrium in the city and let us read this canon

The first reading from the Genesis: (Gen 22: 1-18)

"Now it came after these things that God tested Abraham and said to him…In your seed all the nations of the earth shall be blessed because you have obeyed my voice."

CHAPTER II: *The Fifth Century*

The second reading from Isiah: (Is 61: 1-6)

"The Spirit of the Lord God is upon Me, because the Lord has anointed Me ... But you shall eat the riches of the Gentiles, and in their glory you shall boast."

The third reading from the Acts of the Apostles: (Acts 1: 15-26)

"And in those days, Peter stood in the midst of the brethren... and he was counted among the eleventh apostles."

Psalm 54 response: (Ps 54[55] 22b)

"The words were smoother that oil yet they were drawn swords."

After the psalm, we sit to hear the homily and the catechumens are dismissed.

Having dismissed the catechumens, let us assemble and let us sing this canon.

Ps. 22 Response: "You prepare a table before me in the presence of my enemies." (Ps. 22[23] 5.

A reading from the first Epistle of the Apostle Paul to the Corinthians: (1 Cor. 11: 23-32)

"For I receive from the Lord which I also delivered to you... But when we are judged, we are chastened by the Lord, that we may not be condemned with the world."

The Gospel according to Matthew: (Matthew 26: 17-30)

"And in the first day of the unleavened bread, the disciples drew near Jesus... and they had sung an hymn, they went out into the mount of Olives."

And then, the sacrifice is offered in the saint Martyrium and in front of the holy Cross.

And then we go to the saint Zion.

And then the canon is sung Ps 22 response: (Ps 22[23] 5)

"You prepare a table before me" and the same reading of the Apostle to the Corinthians.

The Gospel according to Mark: (Mark 14: 1-26)

"Now on the first day of the Unleavened Bread... So, His disciples out, and came into the city"

And on the spot we ascended to the mount of Olives and we perform the evening office and we continue to the eve. We pray the psalms three by three, and the prayers are done with prostration.

The first psalm of the gobala 2 (Ps 2:2)[33]

"And the kings of the earth set themselves, and the rulers take counsel together against the Lord and against His Anointed"

For the second gobala the psalm 40 [41]:9)

The third psalm of the gobala the psalm 58 (Ps. 58 [59]:1 "Deliver me, O my God, from my enemies and my persecutors).

For the fourth psalm of the gobala 78(Ps. 108[109] 2-3

The fifth psalm of the gobala: "For the mouth of the wicked and the mouth of the deceitful have opened against me. They have also surrounded me with words.").

After the fifteen psalm and the five gobala and the five prayers, we read the Gospel of John:... (John 13: 21).

---

33 Gobala is a section of Psalm. It is from the Armenian word: գոբաղայ։

CHAPTER II: *The Fifth Century*

At this time of the night, we ascended to the hill
And we sing this response: (Ps 108 [109]: 4)
"In exchange of my love… but I remain in prayer."

The Gospel according to Luke: (Luke 22: 1-65)

"After the feast of unleavened bread… And many other things they blasphemously spoke against him."

At the same hour of the night, we assemble in the place of the disciples, and we read the Gospel according to Mark: "And Jesus said to them… "Before the rooster crows twice, you will deny Me three time." And when he thought about it, he wept." (Mark 1427-72).

"At the hour of the night, we descend from the holy Mount of the Olives at Gethemani and we read the Gospel of Matthew: (Matthew 26: 31-56)

"Then Jesus said to them: "All of you will be made to stumble because of Me this night… But all this was done that the Scriptures of the prophets might be fulfilled." Then all the disciples forsook Him and fled."

And we go the court of the high priest, where Peter repented."

And we read the Gospel of Matthew: (Matthew 26: 57-76).

"And those who laid hold of Jesus led Him away to Caiaphas the high priest… So he went out an wept bitterly."

At this hour of night, we go while singing the psalm 117 with the response: (Ps 117 [118]:1)

"Give thanks unto the Lord, for He is good because His mercy endures forever"

And starting from the door, we say in gobala the psalm 78 until we arrive to the Holy Golgotha et here we read the Gospel of John: (John 18:2-27)

"And Judas who betrayed Him, knew also the place… And again Peter denied Him and on the spot the rooster crows."

The first two readings occur in the ninth hour of Maundy Thursday in the actual lectionary of the Coptic Church.

The third reading and the fourth readings are read in the matins of Maundy Thursday in the actual lectionary of the Coptic Church.

The psalm is used during the Eucharist of the Maundy Thursday.

The Pauline Epistle is still used during the Eucharist of the Maundy Thursday.

The Gospel of Matthew is used during the Eucharist of the Maundy Thursday however the first verses and the last verse is not in the Coptic lectionary.

Only part of the Gospel of Mark is read in the sixth hour of the Maundy Thursday.

The first psalm of Gobala is sung, for the Good Friday eve in the eleventh hour.

The second psalm of the Gobala is not attested in the Coptic lectionary.

The third psalm of the Gobala is used in the sixth hour of Good Friday eve.

The fourth psalm the Gobala is not attested in the Coptic lectionary.

The fifth psalm of Gobala is sung, for the Good Friday eve in the third hour.

The Gospel of John is the reading of the first hour of the Good Friday (the Gospel of the Paraclete).

The readings of the Gospel of Luke are said during the Good Friday eve in the Coptic church.

The readings of the Gospel of Mark are said during the Good Friday eve in the Coptic church.

The readings of the Gospel of Matthew are said during the Good Friday eve in the Coptic church.

The reading the Gospel of John is practiced in the Coptic lectionary in Good Friday eve from the third hour up to the eleventh hour.

The lectionary for the Good Friday[34]

At the dawn, this canon is sung Psalm 108 (Ps 108[109]:4)

---

34 As the readings of the Armenian Lectionary of Jerusalem are too long, we

"For my Love they are my adversaries, but I give myself unto prayer."

And then we read the Gospel according to John:(John 18: 28- 19:16a)

"Then they led Jesus from Caiaphas to the Praetorium … Then he delivered Him to them to be crucified. Then they took Jesus and led Him away."

The reading of the Gospel John of the dawn is used in the Coptic lectionary from the first to the sixth hours.

The morning of the Good Friday

In the morning of Friday, the precious wood of the cross is placed in front of the holy Golgotha. And those who are assembled, adore, and we did the adoration till the sixth hour. At the sixth hour, let us assemble in the holy Golgotha.

And we sing the eight psalms, and eight readings of the prophets, and eight of the Apostle, and the four Gospels and in every psalm, two readings and a prayer once.

Ps 34: (Ps. 34[35] 11)

"For false witnesses have risen against me and ask me things that I do not know."

First reading from the prophet Zachariah: (Zak 11: 11-14)

"Thus, the Cananeans of my flock who were watching me, knew that it was the word of the Lord… Then I cut in tow my other staff, bonds, that I might break the brotherhood between Judah and Israel."

The second reading from the Epistle of Paul to the Galatians: (Gal 6: 14-18)

"I should boast except in the cross of our Lord Jesus Christ.… The grace of our Lord Jesus Christ be with your spirit Amen.".

---

decided to give just the first readings only.

Prayer with song, let us pray the Lord

Psalm 37 response: (Ps 37 [38]: 18 [17])
"For I am ready to fall, and my sorrow is continually before me."

Third reading from Isaiah the prophet: (Is. 3: 9-15)
"Woe to their souls! For they have brought evil upon themselves. They say… What do you mean by crushing My people and grinding the faces of the poor? Says the Lord God of Hosts."

Fourth reading from the epistle of Paul to Philippians:(Philipp 2: 5-11).
"Let this mind be in you which was also in Christ Jesus… and that every tongue should confess that Jesus Christ is Lord, to the glory of God the Father."

Prayer with Response Ps 40 (Ps. 40[41] 7 [8])
"Against me do they devise my hurt".

Firth reading from Isaiah the prophet: (Is. 50: 4-9).
"The Lord has given Me the tongue of the learned that I should know how to speak a word in season to him… Surely the Lord will help Me who is who will condemn Me?"

Sixth reading from the Pauline Epistle to the Romans: (Rom. 5: 6-11).
"For when we were yet without strength in due time Christ died for the ungodly… And not only so, but we also joy in God, through our Lord Jesus Christ, by whom we have now received the atonement."

CHAPTER II: *The Fifth Century*

Psalm with Response: (Ps 21 [22]: 19)

"They divide My garments among them and for My clothing they cast lots."

Seventh reading from Amos the Prophet: (Amos 8: 9-12)

"And it shall come to pass in that day" says the Lord, that I will make the sun go down at noon… They shall run to and for seeking the word of the Lord but shall not find it."

Eighth reading from the Epistle of Paul to the Corinthians: (1 Cor 18-38)

"For the preaching of the cross is to them that perish foolishness but unto us… That as it is written: "He who glorifies, let him glory in the Lord."

Prayer with response: Ps. 30[31] 6 [6])

"Into Your hand I commit my spirit."

Ninth reading of Isaiah the prophet: (Is 52: 13-53:12)

"Behold, my servant shall deal prudently shall exalted and extolled and be very high… Because He poured out His soul unto death, ad He was numbered with the transgressors, and He bore the sin of many, and made intercession for the transgressors."

Tenth reading from the Epistle of Paul to the Hebrew: (Heb. 2: 11-18)

"for both he that sanctifies and they who are sanctified are all of one… For in that he himself has suffered being tempted he is able to succour them that are tempted."

Gospel from the Gospel of Matthew: (Matthew 27:1-56)

"When the morning came, all the chief priest and elders of the people plotted against Jesus…Mary Magdalene, Mary the mother of James and Joses and the mother of Zebedee's sons."

Psalm Response (Ps 68 [69] 22)

"They gave me gall for my food, and for my thirst they gave me vinegar to drink."

Eleventh hour of the prophet of Isaiah: (Is. 63: 1-6)

"Who is this who comes from Edom, … I drunk in My fury, and brought down their strength to the earth."

The reading of the Psalm and the prophecy of Zachariah are read in the Coptic lectionary in the first hour of Good Friday.

The reading of the Pauline Epistle to the Galatians is read in the sixth hour.

The prophecy of Isaiah (third reading) is read in the third hour.

The reading of the Pauline Epistle to the Philippians is read in the ninth hour.

Psalm 40 did not survive in the Coptic rite.

The prophecy of Isaiah is read in the third hour of the Good Friday.

The Pauline Epistle to the Romans does not survive in the Coptic rite.

Psalm 22 is read in the sixth hour.

The prophecy of Amos is read in the sixth hour.

The Epistle of Paul to the Corinthians is read according to some versions of the Coptic Lectionary is read in the first hour of the Good Friday.

Psalm 30 did not survive in the Coptic rite.

The ninth reading, the prophecy of Isaiah 52, is read in the sixth hour of the Coptic lectionary.

The reading of the Epistle of Hebrew did not survive in the Coptic rite.

CHAPTER II: *The Fifth Century*

The reading of the Gospel of Matthew is read in the Lectionary from the first to the eleventh hour in the Coptic lectionary.

Ps 68 [69] 22 is read in the ninth hour.

The prophecy of Isaiah 63: 1-6 is read in the third hour in the Coptic lectionary.

General conclusion

From the comparison between the Armenian Lectionary of Jerusalem and the actual lectionary of the Coptic Church, we find that both texts concord nearly 90%.

We can conclude the roots of the Coptic lectionary are much earlier than what was said before.[35] Even if the revision took place in the thirteenth century, this revision respected the Jerusalemite tradition.

---

35 That means before the reform of the patriarch Gabriel ibn Turaik (1131-1145 AD)

CHAPTER III
THE SIXTH CENTURY

Palm Sunday

In the year 518, Severus of Antioch's 125th homily, of his Cathedral homilies stated that the feasts of the entry of Christ into the temple, the meeting with Simon and Palm Sunday were introduced recently, before they were local feasts celebrated only in Jerusalem.[36]

Trisagion

> "Holy God, Holy Mighty, Holy Immortal
> Who was crucified for us
> Have mercy upon us."

The first part of this hymn was introduced into Byzantine Liturgy of Constantinople by Proclus of Cyzicus[37] who succeeded Nestorius as bishop of Constantinople (431-446 A.D).[38] However a papyrus

---

36   Brière, 1961. p.246[750]-249[753].
37   Proclus was consecrated Bishop of Cyzicus in 426, but not recognized by this city; in 434 he became Patriarch of Constantinople, the second successor of Nestorius, whose heresy he was one of the first to refute in his famous sermon on the Blessed Virgin. Cf. Altaner, 1960, p. 395.
38   Quasten, 1987, p. 728.

from fourth Century preserved in the Collection of the University of Strasbourg includes this Trisagion in the Liturgy of St. Mark.[39]

The second part had been introduced by the Patriarch of Antioch Peter the Fuller (470, 485-489 A.D.)[40] in 471 A.D. as a slogan for those who are opposed to the Council of Chalcedon (i.e. Miaphysites).[41]

This addition was the cause of the riot which took place in November 512 A.D.

We have the same event narrated by the Chalcedonian John Malalas[42] and the anti-Chalcedon Pseudo-Dionysius[43] of Tel Mahre.

Let us see what Malalas wrote first as an eyewitness.

"In his reign (of Anastasius) a civic insurrection took place among the Byzantines in Constantinople over Christian belief because the emperor wanted to add to the *Trisagion* the phrase they use in the eastern cities, "He who was crucified for us, have mercy on us." The population of the city crowded together and rioted violently on the grounds that something alien had been added to the Christian faith. There was uproar in the palace which caused the city Plato to run in, flee and hide from the people anger. The rioters set up a chant, "A new emperor for the Roman state", and went off to the residence of the ex-prefect Marinus the Syrian, burned his house and plundered everything he had, since they could not find him. For he had heard that this great mob of people was coming towards his house and had fled. They claimed that, as an eastern, Marinus had suggested this phrase to the emperor. After plundering his official apartments they cut up his silver with axes and divided it out. They found an eastern monk in the house whom they

---

39   Ibid., p213.
40   Peter the Fuller was a monk in the Monastery of the Sleepless in Constantinople, having views opposed the other monks. He left the Monastery to Antioch. Protected by the Emperor Zeno, he was installed in the seat of Antioch replacing Martyrius. But later, he was exiled. After accepting the Henotikon he returned to Antioch. Cf. Duchesne, 1924, p. 342-357.
41   Stein, 1959, p. 355.
42   John Malalas was born around 490 A.D. He gained a classical education in Antioch. He moved from Antioch to Constantinople in 535 A.D. He was pro-Chalcedon.
43   This work anonymous. It was falsely attributed to the patriarch Dionysius of Tel Mahre (818-845 A.D).

seized and killed and then, carrying his head on a pole, they chanted, "Here is the enemy of the Trinity". They went to the residence of Juliana, a patrician of the most illustrious rank, and chanted for her husband, Areobindus, to be emperor of the Roman state. Areobindus fled and hide in Perama. The emperor Anastasios went up to the *Kathisma* in the hippodrome, without a crown. When the people learned this, they went into the hippodrome. The emperor, through his sacred pronouncement, gained control of the populace of the city, exhorting them to stop murdering and attacking people at random. The whole crowd became quiet and begged him to put on his crown. As soon as they became quiet and stopped forming crowds, the emperor ordered those arrests be made. Of the many brought into custody, he had some punished in this way for many days and after countless numbers had been executed, excellent order and no little fear prevailed in Constantinople and in every city of the Roman state.[44]

The version of Pseudo-Dionysius of Tel Mahre is slightly different being Anti-Chalcedon

"The year 818 (A.D. 506/7); there was a fight and a great riot against Anastasius, because, in accordance with the custom of East, he wanted to add (to the Thrice-holy hymn) 'Thou who wast crucified for us, have mercy upon us" And because of this there were great riots and many killings and plundering of many people in the capital. The emperor Anastasius, being a God-loving (person), wished to add the (formula) Holy art Thou, God, Holy art Thou, Mighty, Holy art Thou, Immortal", the words "Thou who crucified for us have mercy upon us", as the regions of the East and many (other) people did. Now, the whole family of noble Juliana, including herself and the majority of the city, were Nestorians, (Chalcedonians) so when the emperor ordered this, all of Constantinople following the monks of the Sleepless Monastery and others, gathered against him amidst clamour, riot, threat and many protests (and said) 'This (formula) "Thou who crucified for us have mercy upon us", which he wants to introduce to the faith of the Christians, is something new and alien.' Furthermore, they named that robber who was crucified together with our Lord, Dumachos (Demas),

---

44   Jeffreys, Jeffreys, Scott, 1986, Book 16.19, p. 228.

crying out to him, "Thou who wast crucified for us, have mercy upon us" and other rubbish of that kind.

Then they ran and surrounded the palace shouting "Another emperor for Rome." The City prefect, whose name was Plato, had to flee and hide himself from the wrath of the people. But they ran to the house of Marinus the Syrian, the ex-prefect, that is, the regent, to kill him. When (they) learned (that he had managed) to escape from them, they set fire and burned his house, (having) plundered all his possessions. They said that, being a Syrian, he had deceived the emperor into introducing the (formula) "Thou who wast crucified for us, have mercy upon us". So, with axes they broke up his silver in the treasury and divided (it between themselves). Also, on finding in his house a poor Syrian Monk, they killed him; cutting his head and setting it unto a pole they carried it as they rushed around the city, shouting "Here is the conspirator who is the enemy of the Trinity."[45]

The interpolation of this hymn was meant to proclaim, by using an expression from the Nicene-Constantinopolitan Creed, an essential aspect of Cyrillian theology. The Word as the only "subject" in Christ is also the subject of the death "in the flesh" which is "his own": Undoubtedly the *Trisagion* was interpreted as a hymn to the incarnate Word, and the interpolated form of it was formally orthodox. It would have been decidedly heretical had it been addressed to the Trinity, implying the passion of the three persons or the divine essence.[46]

The great theologian Severus of Antioch in his homily on the Annunciation, which was pronounced between 512-513 A.D. (i.e. the same year of the previous riot or few months later) explained clearly the meaning of the Trisagion:

"In fact, some think that when we said the Trisagion, they used to say "Holy God, Holy Almighty, Holy Immortal" and they did not add " Who had been crucified for us." They think that it is an infamy to proclaim immortal who in the flesh had been crucified for us, and they did not learn what Paul said: "But God forbid that I should glory, save in the cross of our Lord Jesus Christ." (Gal 6:14) Hence, the cross is a

---

45 Witakowswki, 1996, p. 7-9.
46 Meyendorff, 1975, p. 35.

real glorification and invincible weapon, when we proclaim this of the incarnated God."[47]

It is important to mention that the Coptic Church addresses this hymn to Christ. For the first stanza, we read *"who was born from the Virgin"* in the last stanza *"Who rose from the dead and ascended to the Heavens "* and thus such a text could be accepted by Chalcedonian and Non-Chalcedonian. Our Church is far from the Heresy of Theopaschiste.

The Troparion O Ⲙⲟⲛⲟⲅⲉⲛⲏⲥ[48]

> "O Only Begotten Son and the Word of God the immortal and everlasting, accepting everything for our salvation, the Incarnated from the Theotokos Ever-Virgin Saint Mary, without change, Christ God becoming Man, crucified, through death treating death, one of the Holy Trinity to whom is glorification with the Father and the Holy Spirit, **Save** us."

This monostrophic well known troparion of the Byzantine Liturgy, which is found also in the Greek Liturgies of St. Mark and St. James;[49] but it does not occur in any of the Three Coptic Liturgies of the Coptic Church. It is sung, however, in the Coptic Church on three other occasions namely at the Consecration of Bishops, the Consecration of the Holy Chrism and the Canonical Hour of Sext on Good Friday.[50]

It contains only one long sentence with one finite verb[51] i.e.: the last word "***save us***" It is true that the hymn-writer of this troparion has selected most of his vocabulary from other sources, and has combined them to form a pattern which also became traditional from the earliest times Yet this is no *random selection and combination,* but one in which

---

47   Brière & Graffin, 1976, p275 [31].
48   Geerard, 1978, Vol III, N°6891 p305. W. Christ-M. Paranikas, «Anthologia Graeca carminum Christianorum, Lipsieae 1971, p52, V. Grumel, «L'auteur et la date de composition du tropaire **o monogenh**»» Echos d'Orient 22, (1923) 398-418.
49   Brightman, 1896, Vol I, p. 33, 116
50   Burmester, 1960, p56 n.6.
51   A finite verb or conjugated verb that means a verb having, person, number, tense, mood, and voice.

a *fine balance* of phrases and sentences is created; in which a definite *pattern of verbal repetition* is cleverly constructed.

This hymn is a compilation the faith Symbols of Nicaea-Constantinople and Chalcedon which could be accepted by both Chalcedonian and non-Chalcedonian Churches.[52]

The text is attributed to either the Monophysite patriarch of Antioch, Severus[53] or to the Emperor Justinian[54]. between 535-536A.D.

In the Coptic church some people attribute this hymn to saint Athanasius the Apostolic but as we can see, the vocabulary is post-Athanasius due to the word "Theotokos". This is because in the time of Athanasius, the main issue was about the Divinity of Christ.[55]

Appendix Of The Troparion

The Troparion "O Only Begotten" is followed by a hymn with the Holy God and an addition. This is called in the Manuscript 106 Liturgy from the Patriarchal Library *hâgiûs.*

> "Holy God who for our sake became Man without change while being God."

> "Holy Mighty who revealed through weakness what is greater than strength."

> "Holy Immortal who was crucified for us and bore death of the Cross and accepted it in His Body while being everlasting and immortal."

> "O Holy Trinity have mercy upon us"

---

52   Barkhuizen, 1984, p3-5.
53   Baumstark, 1958, p93. Maspero, 1923, p104 n11. P.G. CVIII, 477. King, 1948, Vol I, p164.
54   According to George Monachos (the monk) author of the world Chronicle, which runs from Adam to 842 and a good user of John Malalas gave to us his religious standpoint of an anti-iconoclast and mentioned that the author is Justinian. cf. Georgius Monachos, Chronicon C de Boor, Bibliotheca Scriptorum Graecorum et Romanorum Teubneriana, Leipzig 1904, ²ed Wirth Stuttgart1978, Vol II, p627.3.7
55   Müller, 1952. Col. 650.

This form is attested in Liturgy of Upper Egypt. We find many texts in Monastery of Epiphanius,[56] with "Holy God" followed by a petition,[57] or a meditation.[58] We also find a similar text written on an ostracon from the sixth century.[59] These hymns survived in the Coptic Church as it is attested in the Manuscript 106 Liturgy Coptic Patriarchate[60] and Paris Copte 68[61] both from the fourteenth century.

The hymn added to the troparion is the unique witness of this tradition.[62]

The Troparia Of Sext And None Of The Good Friday

> "O Thou Who on the 6th day, at the 6th hour, wast nailed to the Cross, because of the sin which Adam dared (to commit) in the Paradise, tear up the handwriting of our sins, O Christ our God, and deliver us..."

> "O Thou Who didst taste death in the flesh about the 9th hour on account of us, slay our corporal thoughts, O Christ our God and deliver us..."

An examination of the text of the Troporia, and the Theotokia of the Horologion, and Good Friday of the Coptic Church, clearly shows that with the exception of some additions and omissions, it is the same as the Troparia and the Theotokia of the Canonical Hours of the Greek Church. This text occurs sometimes, however, the Troparion and the Theotokion of a Coptic Canonical Hour are not found in the corresponding Greek Hour, but in another Hour.

The Coptic Text has often marked divergence from the actual text of the Greek Horologion. This divergence may possibly be explained by the fact that the Coptic text preserves the form of the Greek text which was current in Egypt at the time when the translation was made. The case of ⲧⲉⲛⲟⲩⲱϣⲧ ⲛ̅ⲧⲉⲕⲙⲟⲣⲫⲏ ⲛⲁⲧⲧⲁⲕⲟ "We worship Thine incorruptible

---

56 Peel, 1991, p. 800b- 802b.
57 Such as for the flood of the Nile cf. MacCoull, 1989, p. 129-135.
58 Such as in our text and cf. **Crum & Evelyn, 1926, n° 603, p. 133.**
59 Di Bitonto Kasser, 1999, p. 93-106.
60 Youhanna Nessim Youssef and U. Zanetti, 2014, p 40.
61 Timbie, 2008, p. 169-178. Davis Schriever and Farag 2020, p134-135.
62 There is another survival of this tradition in the doxology of the heavenly host.cf. Youhanna Nessim Youssef, 2015, pp. 295-305.

form." which the actual Greek text changes ⲙⲟⲣⲫⲏ "Form" to ⲉⲓⲕⲟⲛ= "icon" may well have been made intentionally by iconodules at the time of the Iconoclastic Controversy.[63] It is known the Iconoclastic Controversy started in the VIII Century in Constantinople. Our text should be earlier than the VIII century (perhaps from the VI-VII centuries when the devotion and the prayer started to be addressed to Christ.[64]

The Wednesday Of Job

Job is the figure of Temptation and sadness, which reflects the passion of Christ

In the Cycle of the Holy Week, although Job is not mentioned in this rite. There is an ancient oral tradition that links Job to the Holy Wednesday called in Arabic "اربع ايوب" "the Wednesday of Job."[65] This oral tradition[66] is supported by Manuscript tradition. In fact, some Manuscripts contain a collection of Homilies for the Holy Week which includes four Homilies attributed to John Chrysostom,[67] (These texts should be compared with the Corpus of Leontius of Constantinople)[68] and an apocryphal life[69]

---

63   Burmester, 1973, p. XXVIII-XXXIII.
64   Guillaumont: 1979, p168-183. Kasser, 1996, p. 407-410 Ibid., p 127-134.
65   Sidarus, 1967, p. 1-43 espacialy p11 note 48 and Bibliography p33 N°a14.
66   This practice is not observed in the Rite of the Holy Week nowadays cf. Sidarus, 1969-1970, p. 5-32. It is noteworthy that only the late manuscripts from the XVIII century contain a prophecy from the Book of Job. This could be explained by the fact that the book of Job was read during the Holy Wednesday so there is no need to have prophecies from this Book. For the readings of the Holy Week and the Manuscripts traditions cf. Burmester, 1939, p. 478-479 [430]-[431].
67   cf. Khater and Burmester, 1967, N°48, Lit 33 p15 Lectionary Homilies. Arabic XVIII cent. Fol 1r-12v Story of Job (Wednesday), N°77, Theol 8, p48 Homilies, Arabic XVIII cent 67v-87v The story of Job (probably for the Holy Wednesday). Troupeau, 1974, N°74/10 p. 55 Homily on Job, to be read in the Sext of the Holy Tuesday (cf PG 56, Col 563-567), Simaika and Abd. Al-Masih, Cairo 1942, N° 256, p106, , N° 264 p109, N° 414 p182.
68   cf Allen and Datema, 1991, p. 67-95.
69   Khater and Burmester, 1973, N°119, Hag 2 p57 Vita of Job fol 2r-32r. Troupeau, 1974, N°69/3 p 48 fol. 86r-98 XIV cent., N°107/6 p81 fol. 162-188v. XIV cent. Simaika, 1942, N°616 p277, N°626, p283, N°638, p289, N° 658, p301N°666 p305, N°683, p313.

CHAPTER III: *The Sixth Century*

Only a small allusion to this link survived in the excellent edition of the Euchologion, edited by Hegumen 'Abd al Masih Salib al-Mas'udi al-Baramousi,[70] mentioning: "The priest shall sing with the melody of **Job**[71] **which is the Melody of sadness**" in reference to the Liturgy of Saint Cyril (cf *CPG 5437)*

We do not find elsewhere the mention of the Melody of Job, but the reference to "a melody of sadness" makes us think that this hymn, which has disappeared, was the way to sing the prophecy of Job for the Holy Week - for the Holy Wednesday.

This tradition dates back to VI Century as attested by the homilies of Leontius of Constantinople.

---

70 Zanetti, 1987, p. 407-418.

71 It is interesting to mention that in the edition of Tuki published in 1736 A.D., we find "The priest shall say in the melody of Job" without any explanation, p.286.

CHAPTER IV
THE SEVENTH—EIGHTH CENTURY

The Greek Hymn Of Judas

"Judas lawless who sold Christ to Jews by silver. And the lawless (Jews) took Christ and nailed Him on the Cross at the place called Cranion (Skull)"

The Greek Hymn Of Thief Of The Good Friday

"Remember me, O Lord, when you come in your kingdom..."

According to the linguistic study of the German scholar Baumstark these hymns are from the VII-VIII centuries.[72]

The Hymn Of ⲫⲁⲓ ⲉⲧⲁϥⲉⲛϥ (Fai Etaf-Enf)

"This who offered Himself upon the cross as an acceptable sacrifice for the salvation of our race.

His Good Father smelt Him in the evening time on Golgotha"

This hymn is from the Theotokia of Sunday. We can find the same meaning in Genesis 8:21, Exodus 39:18, Psalm 40:7, Ez. 30:41, Ephesians 5: 2.

---

[72] Baumstark, 1929, p. 76, Robertson, 1990, p. 365-371.

ⲁϥϣⲱⲗⲉⲙ ⲛϫⲉ ⲡϭⲟⲓⲥ ⲫϯ ⲉⲟⲩⲑⲩⲥⲓⲁ ⲟⲩⲟϩ ⲡⲉϫⲉ ⲡ̅ⲟ̅ⲥ̅ ⲫϯ ⲉⲧⲁϥⲙⲟⲕⲙⲉⲕ ϫⲉ ⲛ̄ⲛⲁⲟⲩⲁϩⲧⲟⲧ ϫⲉ ⲥϩⲟⲩⲉⲣ ⲡⲓⲕⲁϩⲓ ⲉⲑⲃⲉ ⲛⲓϩⲃⲏⲟⲩⲓ ⲛ̄ⲧⲉ ⲛⲓⲣⲱⲙⲓ	When the Lord smelt the soothing odour, he said within himself, "Never again will I curse the ground because of the works of man

It is noteworthy that Noah offered this sacrifice after had been rescued from the flood by the Ark ⲕⲩⲃⲱⲧⲟⲥ (kivotos).

The word= ⲕⲩⲃⲱⲧⲟⲥ= "Ark" is also used to express the Ark of the Covenant. The symbolism of this Ark is explained in the Theotokia of Sunday. To support our point of view, we notice that it is followed by either the hymn of ⲧⲁⲓϣⲟⲩⲣⲓ (taishori)= or the hymn of= ⲟⲩⲣⲓ (tishori) which explain that "The censer in the hand of Aaron is the Virgin Mary"

And thus, with few words, the rite of the Coptic Church make allusion to the great sacrifices of the Old Testament of Noah and Aaron and the SACRIFICE[73] of the New Testament i.e. Jesus Christ.

And as we had proven before that the Theotokia[74] is from the seventh or the eighth century, this hymn should also be dated to this period.

---

73 We put this word in capital to highlight the importance of this word.
74 Youhanna Nessim Youssef, 1997, p. 157-170.

CHAPTER V
THE NINTH CENTURY

The Georgian Lectionary[75]

In order to follow the evolution of the readings in the Coptic Church, we possess the Georgian lectionary of Jerusalem which existed in the year 450AD but later amended several times.

The best edition is that published by Tarchnischvili.[76]

The lectionary contains not only the readings but also some hymns.

The readings are more developed and longer than the Armenian Lectionary of Jerusalem.

The Sahidic Lectionary

Only few fragments have survived. These fragments came mainly from the White monastery. Most of these fragments could be dated by the tenth century.

Atanassova compared the pericopes system of the Lectionary of the Sahidic Lectionary with the current Lectionary.[77] This lectionary may have influence on the rite of the Holy Week in the Ethiopian Church.[78]

The topic needs further studies.

---

75   Renoux, 1969, p. 22-23.
76   Tarchnischvili, 1959, p.81-107.
77   Atanassova, "2004, Vol.2 , p.607-620.
78   Zanetti, 1994, p.765-783

CHAPTER VI
THE TENTH CENTURY

The Prayer Of The Foot Washing

The Manuscripts Library of John Rylands in Manchester has a prayer to be said over the basin "without sprinkling the lentils"[79] As per the text, it is said that this prayer is from 'the book of Joseph',[80] presumably either the owner of the book copied or the author of some liturgical work[81]

"Blessed art Thou, Lord, God, Almighty, the Father of our Lord and our Saviour, Jesus Christ Who spoke first by the mouth of His holy prophets; Who did redeem the race of man from the bitter slavery of the devil by the coming of Thy Only Begotten Son in flesh, our Lord Jesus Christ; Who showed us how to bear His cross and to tread upon serpents and scorpions, Who granted us the remission of our sins by the purifying of a second birth. He taught His holy Mystery though our Lord Jesus Christ, who gave it to His disciple. After the supper and laid aside his garments and took a towel, and girded himself, and started to wash the disciples' feet and to wipe with a towel wherewith he was girded. He said to them, Know ye what I have done to you? Ye call me Master and Lord and ye say well; for so I am. If I then have washed

---

79 . See the Macrizi's report.
80 See the Macrizi's report about the Maundy Thursday.
81 Crum, 1909 p. 9 N°24.

your feet, ye also ought to wash one another's feet. I have given to you the example when I did so.

For this, O Lord, Jesus Christ, grant this to us and make us inherit with the Holy Apostles by the Grace."

It seems that this prayer is an old prayed addressed to God the Father through the Son. The prayers addressed directly to the Son appeared only in the Seventh century. The actual used prayer is directly addressed to the Son. This type of prayer appeared in the seventh century while earlier prayers are addressed to God the Father through the Son, hence, we can conclude that this form of prayer is earlier than what is used nowadays.[82]

The Dialect of this prayer is not a pure Sahidic, it seems that this prayer belongs to a local tradition. Especially the mentioning of "without sprinkling the lentils" which shows that there was a tradition in a precise time by sprinkling the lentil.

---

[82] قارن عطالله ارسانيوس. كتاب اللقان و السجده. القاهره 1971 .ص106-107 حيث هناك تشابه مع هذه الصلاة.

For this prayer cf. Atallah Arsenius al-Muharraqi, the book of the Basin and the genuflection, Cairo 1971, p.106-107.

CHAPTER VII
THE ELEVENTH CENTURY

Under the Patriarchs of Alexandria, Christodulos (1047-1077 A.D.), Cyril II (1078- 1092 A.D.), Gabriel II (1131-1146 A.D.) and Cyril III (1235-1243 A.D.), many new important laws were added to the Coptic Canon Law. The first of this series of new canons was promulgated by Christodulos, 66th patriarch, at Alexandria on Sunday 8th of Misri, A.M. 764 (1st. August 1048).

Two of these Canons deal with the Rite of the Holy Week

> Canon 8 - And after the completion of the Liturgy (Quddas) on the Sunday of Olives (Palm Sunday) there shall be read the gospel and the Diptych for the dead after the Apostle (the lesson from the Pauline Epistles) of Paul appointed for the dead, and after this there shall be read over the assembly of the people the Absolution, because in Holy Week neither Absolution nor the diptych nor the burial service is allowed until the Feast of Easter is completed.

> Canon 9- On Maundy Thursday the Liturgy (Quddas) shall be (celebrated) in fear and trembling and quietness without either Kiss (of Peace) or the hand touching (At the Kiss of Peace the members of the Congregation touch one another' hands) and the Prosphorin[83] shall not be said, but instead

there shall be said Meta phobou[84] without the Absolution either at the beginning or at the end.

And the Liturgy (Quddas) of Holy Saturday there shall be said the diptych and the Absolution, but there is not the Kiss."[85]

---

84 With fear
85 Burmester, 1932, p. 71-84.

CHAPTER VIII
THE TWELFTH CENTURY

In this century, Abû al-Makarim wrote his book about Churches and Monasteries in Egypt.[86]

Palm Sunday in the Church of Haret Zuwylah

"The priest and the laity of that church are accustomed to assemble in church on the feast of the Olive every year, where they pray in the early morning. Then they come out of the church to the street in which that church stands carrying the olive branches, the Bible, the crosses, the censers, and the tapers, where they pray and read the Bible. They pray on behalf of the Caliph and his vizier. Then they return to the Church to spend the rest of the day and leave. They repeat the same rites on the second and the third days of the feast, the feast of the Cross of the Nile is also celebrated on the seventeenth of Thot every year.

All those feasts were abolished in the dynasty of al-Ghuzz and al Kurds in the year 565 A.H. (1169 A.D.)"[87]

---

[86] Our references refer to the edition of Samuel al-Suriani, 1984, 4 Vol., and also Evetts and Butler, 1895. For specific studies cf. Samuel al-Suriani, 1990, p78. (For codicology and Composition) Zanetti, 1995, p. 85-133. (For the Authorship and Influence) Den Heijer, 1993, p. 209-219. (Social study of the Delta) Martin, 1997, p181-199. Id., 1998, p. 45-49, Id., 2000, p. 83-92; Id., 2004, p. 313-320. Youssef, 1998-1999, p. 45-54.

[87] Samuel al-Suriani, 1984, fol 4 b.

The Palm Sunday in Alexandria

"The procession of the Olive (Palm Sunday) started at night in the city. They used to cross the city from the Church of St. Sergius (Abû Sergah) to the church of Soter (the Saviour) with supplication and reading. But Muslims attacked this tradition and caused many troubles, preventing it for 25 years. Then the procession of the Olive (Palm Sunday) reappeared during the reign of Mizwa in the year 444 A.H (1053 A.D.) in the patriarchate of Christodulos, the sixty sixth in the order of succession and appeared during the reign of al Aamir. That rite continued for many years and was abolished in the dynasty of al-Ghuzz and the Kurds in the year 565 (1169A.D.)"[88]

---

88   Samuel al-Suriani, 1984, fol 82a,b.

CHAPTER IX

THE THIRTEENTH- FOURTEENTH CENTURY

Guide[89] of the beginners and the instruction of the Laymen

This book was compiled by an anonymous around the thirteenth century. According to the study of Fr. Misael al-Baramusi,[90] the most ancient manuscript is Baramus 9 and Vatican. We find a description of the rite of the Holy Week.[91]

> On the eve of Palm Sunday, they start the prayer as usual, the Theotokia with its tune, and they read the tarh in the Palm Sunday tune, and they continue the prayer as usual.
>
> They offer the mass as usual and they sing the psalm for the Gospel of Matthew as usual, and the psalm of the Gospel of John in the Singari tune. The Gospel of John is for the celebrant priest. The celebrant priest recites the liturgy of St Gregory. When they finish the Gospel and the mass, they do not read psalm 150 but instead they read the funerary service for men with the tune of sadness, and after that, the funerary service for women and children. They read the absolution and the people are dismissed.

---

89   For these books cf. Misael al Baramusi, 2022, p. 23-107.
90   Misael al Baramusi, 2020, p.24-25.
91   Misael al Baramusi, 2020, p. 102-107.

Then, they (the people) assemble on the eve of the Palm Sunday in the church outside the chorus- for the Lord suffered outside the city- and start the prayer from outside as arranged by the father the patriarch Anba Gabriel ibn Turaik (1131-1145AD) which is: ⲑⲱⲕ ⲧⲉ ϯϫⲟⲙ[92] 12 times, the prophecies and the translation, the Gospels, the Tarh in the tune of sadness and if there is homily of John Chrysostom or another author as usual then the priest read the supplications and k̄ⲉ ⲉⲗⲉⲏⲥⲟⲛ [93] 40 times and the mimar of the Palm Sunday.

They continue this rite day and night to the Matins of Thursday, they read the prophecies as usual outside, then the priest opens the door of the sanctuary, which is veiled with a blue or black veil. He (the priest) says the prayer of Thanksgiving and offers the incense. The deacons recite ⲧⲁⲓϣⲟⲩⲣⲏ[94] then he reads the Acts with the special tune, and sing Agios with the tune of the crucifixion, and the priest recites the litany of the Gospel and the psalm with the tune of sorrow. Afterwards, they close the door of the sanctuary and they recite the tarh and litanies in the place of the Pascha outside, and Kyrie Eleison and the blessing as usual, and the prayer of the ninth hour as usual, then they fill the basin with water and they pray before commencing the liturgy.

This is what is established in the church now fearing that something happens to the bread and the wine, the high priest starts with the prayer of the Basin, he recites the prayer of Thanksgiving and offers the incense. The people say psalm 50, they read the prophecies and their translation, and the Pauline Epistle using the yearly tune. The priest says the litanies included in the book of the Pascha concerning the Basin.

They continue the prayer, and he (the priest) washes the feet of the congregation and their hands and faces. The water is distributed, and he (the priest) enters to the sanctuary. And

---

92   Thok te tigom= to You is the power
93   Kyrie eleyson= Lord have mercy.
94   Taišuri= this censer.

CHAPTER IX: *The Thirteenth- Fourteenth Century*

only the Pauline Epistle is read -no Catholicon or Praxis. They sing Agios using the yearly tune, neither the sorrowful nor the joyful.

No one kisses the Gospel because of the kiss of Judah, the priest does not recite the Aspasmos [95]nor the diptych. The psalm 150 is not sung but instead the prophecies, the psalm, and the Gospel of the Pascha with the sorrowful tune. The priest does not dismiss.

Good Friday, the church is adorned with curtains, seven or three censer are prepared and put in front of the icon of the crucifixion with three crosses. They pray the third hour as usual.

In the sixth hour after reading the prophecies, the priests offer incense according to their ranks and they read the Pauline epistle with the tune of sorrow, and sing Agios Dimas, and Agios with tune of the crucifixion with "who was crucified" three times, the psalm with the Adribi tune, and the deacon reads the Gospel. The tarh is read as usual. The priest recites the litanies and finishes the prayer. They turn the lights off and they sing the hymn of the good thief which is ⲙⲛⲏⲥⲟⲏⲧⲓ[96] they say it in Arabic and the mimar of the good thief to the ninth hour as usual.

The twelfth hour, the prophecies are read in Coptic and Arabic and they light the candles, they carry the crosses and the icons of the crucifixion, they go up to the sanctuary and they sing the psalm and the Gospel from the Ambon and the tarh from the navel. The priest says the litanies and he raises the cross and the people say 400 Kyrie Eleison, to the East 100, to the West 100, to the North 100 and to the South 100 and then 10 with the long tune and the deacons sing ϩⲓⲧⲉⲛ ⲡⲉⲕⲥ̅ⲧ̅ⲥ̅[97]. They enter the sanctuary and they place the icon in a prosferin[98] under the altar with roses and they say

---

95	Greeting
96	Mnistit = remember me
97	Hiten pekstavros = through your cross.
98	altar cloth

ⲡ̄ⲟ̄ⲥ ⲡ̄ⲟ̄ⲥ[99] then they read the 150 psalms. They read on the eve of Tuesday the Gospel of Matthew, the eve of Wednesday the Gospel of Mark and eve of Thursday the Gospel of Luke and the eve of Friday the Gospels of the Paraclete and so on. Saturday the psalms are read and the eve of Sunday.

The rite of the bright Saturday

Having finished the psalms, the high priest concludes with psalm 151 and the archdeacon continues with ⲁⲛⲟⲕ ⲡⲉ ⲡⲓⲕⲟⲩϫⲓ[100] The people form the procession, then the people sit in the nave of the church and the high priest goes up to the cathedra and they sing hymns, read (the story of) the golden statue and they translate the story of Susanna.

The altar is covered by a white or blue cover and the high priest recites the prayer of thanksgiving then the priests offer the incense, and they say the litany for the dead and the hymn of the angels, no one should kiss the hand of the priest.

The priest starts ⲁϥϯ ⲙ`ⲡⲟⲩⲛⲟϥ[101] and the theotokia and the Lobš up to the širyat[102] with the yearly tune ⲡⲓⲕⲃⲉⲣⲛⲓⲧⲏⲥ[103] and the doxology to the end of ⲡⲉⲛⲟ̄ⲥ̄ ⲓⲏⲥ [104] then the ⲧⲉⲛϭⲓⲥⲓ ⲙⲙⲟ[105], the Creed up to 'He was crucified' and Kyrie Eleyson while processing around the church. No one kisses the icon or the Gospel. The Pauline epistle is read half in the sorrow tune and the other with the joyful tune and then Agios. The psalm in two tunes one of sorrow and the other one in joyful tune. The same applies for the Gospel then the tarh which is ⲁⲩⲉϣ ⲡⲉⲛⲥⲱ̄ⲣ[106] the priest continues as usual and they read the canon ⲡ̄ⲟ̄ⲥ ⲡ̄ⲟ̄ⲥ.

---

99   Pchois pchois= Lord Lord
100   Anok pe pikouji= I am the least.
101   Afti mpounof= He gave joy to us. *the Psali of Saturday."
102   Hail.
103   This is the begining of the doxology of Severus of Antioch which is the standard of the yearly tune
104   Penchois isous = Our Lord Jesus : the conclusion of the Theotokia Batos
105   Tenchsi mmo-= we praise you. The introduction to the creed
106   Aveš pensoter= they crucified our Saviour

CHAPTER IX: *The Thirteenth- Fourteenth Century*

Before the 6ᵗʰ (of January) on that day which is the bright Saturday the people assemble to the church, they prepare 7 candles and seven censers, and they read the Apocalypse which is the Revelations of John the Evangelist.

They continue the liturgy they say the three litanies, the creed up to 'buried' which is in Coptic ⲟⲩⲟ⳽ ⲁⲩⲕⲟⲥ⳽, no Aspasmos but the litany for the reposed and at the end of the mass they do not read the psalm 150 but the psalm 21 Ⲡⲁⲛⲟⲩϯ Ⲡⲁⲛⲟⲩϯ[107] with is tune.

After communion, the priest does not say the dismissal.

Lectionary

The British Library holds the most ancient Complete Lectionary of the Holy Week, Manuscript N Add. 5997 dated A.M. 990 (1273 AD).[108] This manuscript contains the Rite of Feet washing which was published as the second rite in the edition of Attallah Arsenius al-Moharraqi,[109] Scriptures pericopes and Exhortations.[110]

From this century, we possess the Codex Scaligeri which is a bilingual Greek-Arabic manuscript copied in 1265 in a Scetis monastery, (Wadi Natrun). It presents a rather less voluminous rite.[111]

According to the tradition of the Coptic Church the Holy Week Lectionary was compiled by the Patriarch Gabriel II (1131-1145 A.D.) with the help of the monks of the Monastery of St. Macarius. Further lessons and also a number of short homilies or exhortations were afterwards added to the Lectionary by a certain Peter, bishop of Behnasa.[112] However

---

107   Panouti Panouti -= My God my God
108   Burmester, 1933, p. 173-294, 25/2, p179485.
109   But unfortunately, it is not in use anymore. Even the popular edition of al-Mahaba Bookshop, Fagallah, and Alexandria did not mention it. For the edition of this rite cf. Malak, 1964, p1-35 in particular N°XXI, p22-23.
110   Burmester, 1934, p. 21-70.
111   Zanetti, 2003, p131.
112   Burmester, 1934, p. 21-70.

this tradition contradicts another documented event in the life of this Patriarch which is recounted in the *History of the Patriarchs of the Egyptian Church*[113]

"He (Gabriel) went up to the Monastery of Saint Macarius for his consecration there, as had been the custom for those patriarchs before him. A conversation took place regarding the meaning of the 'Confession' which is said over the Oblation before communicating from it, and it is: "I believe and I confess that this is the Body of our Lord and our Saviour Jesus Christ Which He took from the God-bearer, my Lady Mary the Virgin, and It became one with His Divinity" Some of the monks at the mentioned Monastery refused to accept the wording of this expression which is "It became one with His Divinity", because it (had been) added, and they mentioned that it was not their custom to say it… There occurred on account of these troubles and discussions. At the end, it was decided to add the other words which they agreed to join to it and they are: "It became one with His Divinity without confusion and without mingling "

If it was so just for adding **one word to the Holy Mass**, we can expect greater reactions if the Patriarch "dared" to innovate a new book. On the other hand, the History of the Patriarchs would also mention this event.

In the fourteenth century, Ibn Kabar mentioned a different system to read the Bible during the Holy Week in the Monastery of St. Macarius. So, it would be amazing if the monks of this Monastery prepared the Lectionary and did not use it.

To conclude, we have the most **ancient Lectionary** from the thirteenth century, and in the fourteenth century Peter of Behnasa added new lessons. But it is hard to believe that Gabriel II created or compiled this book, it is more likely that this patriarch approved a local tradition and ordered to generalize it rather than created a new liturgical Book.

---

113   Khater & Burmester, 1968, p. 42-43.

CHAPTER IX: *The Thirteenth- Fourteenth Century*

Turuhat[114]

It is difficult enough to know the history of a Coptic Liturgical Rite,[115] for some of them had been written first in Greek and translated after that to Coptic and to Arabic, and the others had been directly written in Coptic.

A linguistic study will be useless to determine the age of a Coptic Liturgical Book for most of the vocabulary is taken from the Scriptures. On the other hand, most of the Manuscripts are recent and do not reflect the time of redaction.[116]

It is important to mention that the Book of Turuhat has its first edition in 1914 and has been reprinted many times after [117]

The Turuhat are based on the Old Testament readings and always follow the actual reading and not the ancient tradition[118]

as preserved in the manuscript British 5997add. published by Burmester and dated 1273 AD.[119]

---

114   Turuhat is the plural of Tarh: This is a variable hymn containing explanations of the Gospel, or the prophecies for the Holy Week. (During the liturgical year, it is a text praising the saints or the feast)

115   Coquin, 1989, p. 210.

116   The liturgical manuscripts are quickly consumed as they are used daily. Deterioration includes wax stains, dust etc… They are recopied and we cannot know the age of the text as most of the copies are recent.

cf. Störk, 1995, p. 504 N°248 Hymn. 85, from 17/18 century, p627 N° 319 Varia 10, from 16/17 century.

117   القمص فيلوثاوس المقاري و المعلم ميخائيل جرجس: 1914. 255 صفحة
القمص عطالله ارسانيوس المحرقي. 1969. طبعة ثانية 264 صفحة.

ⲡⲓϫⲱⲙ ⲛ̄ⲧⲉ ⲡϫⲓⲛⲕⲱϯ ⲙ̄ⲡⲓϣⲁⲓ ⲛ̄ⲧⲉ ⲡⲓⲥ̅ⲧⲁⲩⲣⲟⲥ ⲛⲉⲙ ⲫⲁ ⲡⲓϣⲁⲓ ⲛ̄ⲧⲉ ⲛⲓⲃⲁⲓ ⲛⲉⲙ ⲛⲓⲧⲁⲗⲓⲁ ⲛ̄ⲧⲉⲡⲓϩⲙⲉⲉⲟⲩ ⲛⲉⲙ ⲛⲁ ⲡⲓⲛ̅ ⲛ̄ⲉϩⲟⲟⲩ ⲉ̅ⲑ̅ⲩ̅ ⲕⲁⲧⲁ ϯⲉⲕⲕⲗⲏⲥⲓⲁ ⲉ̅ⲑ̅ⲩ̅ ⲛ̄ⲣⲉⲙⲛ̄ⲭⲏⲙⲓ ⲛ̄ⲟⲣⲑⲟⲇⲟⲝⲟⲥ

مطرانية بني سويف
دورة عيدي الصليب و الشعانين و طروحات البصخة المقدسة والخمسين حسب ترتيب الكنيسة القبطية -الارثوذكسية
القاهرة 1983. 428صفحة.

This edition is a compilation of three liturgical books. The Coptic Title shows only the first book i.e. the Book of procession.

118   As we mentioned above, we have the reading of the manuscript British Museum 5997 which contains some reading different from the actual reading

119   Burmester, 1933, p169-294; Id. 1939, p. 175-485.

It is also known that Peter bishop of Behnasa, (thirteenth-fourteenth century) revised the reading of the Holy week lectionary. [120]

It seems that this bishop took some texts adopted in the Upper Egyptian tradition and integrated them in the Turuhat as Maria Cramer had demonstrated by comparing some of the Turuhat with the Ms 575 in the Pierpont Morgan Library in New York which is dated 893AD. [121]

Dr. O.H. Burmester had published a description of the Turuhat in the Coptic Church, where he clearly demonstrated, by comparing some of the Sahidic texts of the Antiphonation preserved in the collection of the Pierpont Morgan Ms 575 in the Pierpont Morgan Library in New York which is dated 893AD. [122] with the Bohairic Turuhat, that some Turuhat were written before the ninth century.[123] It seems that Peter, bishop of Behnasa, took some texts adopted in the Upper Egyptian.

Burmester also published the most Ancient Manuscript of the Bohairic Lectionary date 1273 A.D. which does contain many pericopes.[124] We may notice that the Turuhat explain many pericopes of the Old testament such as the matins of the Holy Monday,[125] (concerning the first chapter of Genesis), the none of Monday of the Holy week[126] (concerning the first chapters of Genesis), the matins of the Tuesday of the Holy Week (concerning Exodus),[127] and the sext of the night of Maundy Thursday (concerning Isaiah).[128] The tierce,[129] sext[130] and none[131] of Maundy Thursday and the tierce of Good Friday.[132]

---

120   Burmester, 1937, p. 78-10, p. 505-549.
121   Cramer, 1965, p. 90-115; especially p. 93-94.
122   Cramer, 1965, p. 90-115; especially p 93-94.
123   Burmester, 1937, p. 78-109. Id., 1937, p. 505-549.
124   Burmester, 1939, p. 175-485
125   القمص فيلوثاوس. كتاب طروحات البسخة المقدسة. ص.41-45.
126   Ibid p54-68.
127   bid p 91-95.
128   Ibid. p155.
129   Ibid. p169-172.
130   Ibid. p172-174
131   Ibid. p174-180.
132   Ibid. p212-215.

CHAPTER IX: *The Thirteenth- Fourteenth Century*

The Turuhat always follow the actual reading even when there is divergence with the Manuscript Add 5997 British Museum regarding the reading of the sext, none and eleventh hours of the eve of Wednesday.

It is quite clear that the Turuhat had been compiled after the reform of Peter of Behnasa in the thirteenth-fourteenth century[133]

It seems that bishop took some texts already known from Upper Egyptian Manuscripts and included them in the Book of Turuhat, hence, we find some similarities between the Tarh of the Palm Sunday and the Manuscript 575 fol. 106 from Pierpont Morgan New York.[134]

We can conclude that the Turuhat go back to the thirteenth -fourteenth century after the reforms of Peter of Behnasa, as we find explanations of the prophecies. We may notice that, as the Coptic language ceased to be used as daily language, some irregularities in the Coptic such as in the word: ⲡⲓⲥⲟⲛ ⲃ̄.[135]. The definitive article should be omitted and to make it ⲥⲟⲛ ⲃ̄.

This use became the rule by the fourteenth century, in the time of Ibn Kabar (see below) when the tarh of the Bright Saturday explains the events of the twelfth hour of the Good Friday.[136]

---

133   Burmester, 1937, p. 235-254 especially p. 236-237.
134   Cramer, 1965, p. 90-115 especially p 93-94.
135   Philotheus, op.cit., p21.
136   Muyser, 1952, p. 175-184.

CHAPTER X
THE FOURTEENTH CENTURY

In this century, we get two detailed descriptions of the trite of the Holy Week

Ibn Kabar

Shams al Riasah Abû al-Barakat Ibn Kabar (1324 A.D.)[137] wrote his book *Lamp of Darkness for the explanation of the (liturgical) Service*"[138] In the time of Ibn Kabar, churches were closed, so he felt that he should provide a detailed description for the future generation. We used here. the oldest copies of this book (from Paris dated to 1363 A.D and Upsalla dated 1546 A.D but copied from another Manuscript dated 1357 A.D.)

What we observe for the feast of the Palm Sunday[139]

We pray the Asheya (Vespers) in the night of Lazarus Saturday. We sing using the same tunes as the feast of the Cross. We

---

137   for this author cf. Coquin, 1966 col. 1349-1351. Samir Khalil, 1978, p. 179-188. Atiya, 1991, p. 1267-1268. Samir Khalil, 2000, p. 629-655.

138   Only few chapters had been published scientifically cf. Villecourt, 1923 252-253. Id., 1928 p. 575-734.

There are also three popular editions the first is done by deacon Ayoub El Cheikh in 1951, (the first six chapiters). The second by R.P. Samir Khalil S.J. (the first 12 chapters -the first part) The second part had been edited by Mgr Samuel according to the Manuscript of Deir El Sourian. en 1992

139   Villecourt, 1925, p. 269-273.

sing a hymn (Tarh) of the above-mentioned feast which is
ⲙⲁϣⲉⲛⲁⲕ ϩⲓϫⲉⲛ ⲟⲩⲧⲱⲟⲩ ⲉⲧϭⲟⲥⲓ (mashenak hijen ou-to-ou et-chosi)

We recite the whole psalmodia and we process the olive branches around the Church. We prepare the olive branches and the palm. We stop in front of the altars, the icons, and every time we stop in a place, we sing the Psalm and the Gospel in Coptic in addition to some hymns and the Tarh of the Feast with the tune of the Cross.[140]

Some do this after the Psalmodia and before the matins, some others do this after the matins and before the prayer of the Gospel.[141] The readings of the Gospel while we process the palm are different from a church to another.

The Custom in the Church of Muallaqah in Misr (Old-Cairo), is to read the section concerning Zaccheus from Luke in front of the icon of the Palm Sunday; the section concerning the end of the world in front of the icon of John Baptist, the section concerning his memory in front of the house of women,[142] the section of the centurion from Luke, the Annunciation in front of the icon of Our Lady, in front of the altar of Michael the section of the negociant from Matthew and near the Baptistery we read the section of blessed Mary.

In the Monastery of Shahran, they used to read suitable section in front of each icon and in everywhere in the Monastery and near the altars. Near the kitchen the section of the five loaves and the seven loaves, near the tombs, they used to read the reading of the burial section etc.

In the Monastery of Saint Macarius, the custom is to have a palm procession in and out the Monastery.

---

140   We translate the text as is, without changing.

141   Which is observed nowadays.

142   The women used to stay in the second floor in order not to mix with men. This is called the house of women. Women were only allowed to descend in the first floor in the early twentieth century, with the building of the church of Boutrosia in Abbasia. Cf. Coquin, 1974, p.65-80.

CHAPTER X: *The Fourteenth Century*

The people of Upper Egypt, have the *ermenia* and dogmata,[143] composed from the psalms of David which are mentioned in a book called El-Kafus.[144] They choose parts from the psalms and they sing according to the place where they pass, river, sand, hill, green grass, tree and other things.

Here is the tradition of the Egyptians (those of Old Cairo) they return with the Olive to the main altar. They pray the prayer of the Gospel, and they sing the psalm and hence they finish the matins and offer the Mass. It is not the Liturgy of Cyril which should be read but the Liturgy of St. Gregory or St. Basil. The best is St. Gregory, which is more suitable for the feasts of our Lord. When they finished the Mass and while partaking of the communion, they did not say the psalm 150 but the funerary sections, section by section: the Epistle of Paul, the Psalms, the Gospels of funerary until the end of communion.

The reason for this is during the Holy Week the funerary services are suspended in the Church, only a reading from the Pentateuch is read. Hence, the Fathers had instituted these prayers during the Palm Sunday. We read the whole or a part of the service, according to the time.

Starting from Asheya we observed the rite of the Holy Week.

The Rite of Monday Tuesday and Wednesday[145]

For Monday, Tuesday and Wednesday, their night rite is identical. That is: for each prayer we read the pericopes of the Prophets and the Arabic translation and then Kyrie Eleyson. ⲐⲰⲔ ⲦⲈ ϮϪⲞⲘ ⲚⲈⲘ ⲠⲒⲰⲞⲨ ⲚⲈⲘ ⲠⲒⲤⲘⲞⲨ ⲒⲆ̅[146] 12 times). We sing the psalm with the tune of sadness and the Gospel with the tune of sadness and then are read in Arabic.

---

143   Hermenia and dagmata are two types of hymns from the Upper-Egyptian tradition, which are not used anymore.
144   cf Youssef, 1998, p. 121-134.
145   Villecourt, 1925, p. 277-280.
146   thok te tigom nem pi-o-ou nem pi-esmou = to You is the power, glory and blessing

For the interpretation, when we read the psalm and after this to be worthy to hear the Holy Gospel; "Our Lord, our God, have mercy upon us and make us worthy to hear the Holy Gospel " a Chapter from the Gospel of ... the evangelist... And when it is finished, we read the Tarh of the hour. And if there is a sermon, it will be read after the Gospel.

And we read the=Τⲱⲃϩ and the reader says before: ⲕⲗⲓⲛⲟⲙⲉⲛ ⲅⲟⲛⲟⲩ ⲁⲛⲁⲥⲧⲟⲙⲉⲛ ⲅⲟⲛⲟⲩ ⲕⲉ ⲁⲛⲁⲥⲧⲟⲙⲉⲛ[147]

(four times) and the people make 12 prostrations except of the first and the third prayer of the night because they follow the break of fast.

The priest or an archdeacon read them. They are 18 ⲧⲱⲃϩ.

ⲧⲱⲃϩ ϩⲓⲛⲁ ⲛⲧⲉ ⲫϯ ⲛⲁⲓ ⲛⲁⲛ	Pray for the God have mercy upon us
ⲃ̄ ⲡⲓⲥⲉⲙⲛⲓ ⲙⲡⲁⲓⲧⲟⲡⲟⲥ ⲉ̄ⲑ̄ⲩ̄ ⲫⲁⲓ	and the establishment of this holy place[1]
ⲅ̄ ⲛⲏⲉⲧϣⲱⲛⲓ ⲛⲧⲉ	The ill of
ⲇ̄ ⲛⲉⲛⲓⲟϯ ⲛⲉⲛⲥⲛⲏⲟⲩ ⲉⲧⲁⲩϣⲉ ⲉⲡϣⲉⲙⲙⲟ	Our fathers and our brethren who traveled abroad
ⲉ̄ ⲉϫⲉⲛ ⲛⲓⲕⲁⲣⲡⲟⲥ	for the fruits
ⲋ̄ ⲛⲧⲉ ⲫϯ ⲑⲏⲓⲧⲉⲛ	In order that God give us
ⲍ̄ ⲛⲉⲛⲓⲟϯ ⲛⲉⲙ ⲛⲉⲛⲥⲛⲏⲟⲩ ⲉⲧⲁⲩⲉⲛⲕⲟⲧ	Our fathers and our brethren who died
ⲏ̄ ⲛⲏⲉⲧϭⲓⲣⲱⲟⲩϣ	for those who are in charge
ⲑ̄ ϯⲟⲩⲓ ⲙⲙⲁⲩⲁⲧⲥ ⲉ̄ⲑ̄ⲩ̄	The only Unique Holy[2]
ⲓ̄ ⲡⲉⲛⲓⲱⲧ ⲉ̄ⲑ̄ⲩ̄ ⲡⲁⲧⲣⲓ	Our father the holy patri[3]
ⲓ̄ⲁ̄ ⲛⲧⲉ ϯⲁⲅⲓⲁ ⲛⲉⲕⲕⲗⲏⲥⲓⲁ	For the Holy Church
ⲓ̄ⲃ̄ ⲛⲉⲛⲭⲓⲛⲑⲱⲟⲩϯ ⲉϧⲟⲩⲛ ⲫⲁⲓ	For those who are assembled here[4]
ⲓ̄ⲅ̄ ⲛⲧⲉ ⲟⲩⲟⲛ ϣⲉⲡϧⲓⲥⲓ ⲛⲧⲱⲟⲩ	For those who suffer[5]
ⲓ̄ⲇ̄ ⲛⲏⲉⲧϩⲟⲭϩⲉϫ ⲛⲉⲙⲛⲏⲉⲧϧⲉⲛ ⲛⲓϣⲧⲉⲕⲱⲟⲩ	for those who suffer from the prisons

---

147 Clinomen gonou anastomen gonou kai anastomen – bow knee = raise and bow knee and raise

ĪE ϮΨΥΧΗ ΝΙΒΕΝ ΕΤΑΥΘΩΟΥϮ	For everybody present[6]
ĪS̄ ΕΧΕΝ ΟΥΟΝ ΝΙΒΕΝ ΕΤΑΥϨΟΝϨΕΝ	For everybody who ordered [7]
ĪZ̄ ΕΧΕΝ ΠΧΙΝΜΟϢΙ	for the raising up[8]
ĪΗ ΕΧΕΝ ΠΙΠΑⲤΧΑ ΕΘΥ	For this Holy= Pascha[9]

Some priests say only 12 litanies.

Then ΦϮ ΝΑΙ ΝΑΝ (efnouti nai nan) (God have mercy on us) and Kyrie Eleyson 48 (times) stanza by stanza: concluded by the Lord's prayer, and the priest say these words in Coptic ΑΡΙ ΑΓΑΠΗ ΚΩΛΧ ΝΝΕΤΕΝΑΦΗΟΥΙ ΝΤΕΤΕΝϬΙ ΜΠΙⲤΜΟΥ ΠϬⲤ ΕΡΕ ΠΟΥⲤΜΟΥ ΕΡΩΤΕΝ

(Ari tiagapi, kolg enetenaphioui ntechi pismou Pchois, ere pousmou eroten)

"Make charity, bow your heads in order to receive the blessing of the Lord, May the Lord bless you." And after, he said the benediction, he dismissed the people saying: ΜΑϢΕΝΩΤΕΝ ϦΕΝ ΟΥϨΙΡΗΝΗ ΟΥΟϨ ΘΩΟΥϮ ΕϮΑΓΙΑ ΝΕΚΚΛΗⲤΙΑ ϦΕΝ ΑΧΠ ΝΙΜ ΝΕΜΩΤΕΝΚ

The prophecies in the Church of Egypt (Old Cairo) are arranged for the matins and the none of the days only and some hours for the night. *For the Passover at Sadamant*, the prophecies are arranged for every hour of day and night.[148]

The reading of the sermons is a general habit, but only for the Matins and the None of the days because the assembly of the people during these two hours.

And if the Patriarch is present and he is able to read, he reads the first prophecy of the first hour of Monday, the associated Gospel, the Gospel of the none of the day of Tuesday (which is the section of Sandaliyah), and the first prophecy of the first hour of Wednesday. During the night of Tuesday, we read the Gospel of Matthew and during the night of Wednesday the Gospel of Mark and during the night of Thursday the Gospel of Luke.

---

148   Which is the actual rite in the Coptic Church.

What is observed for the Maundy Thursday

For the Matins we read a chapter from the Law and after that ⲑⲱⲕ ⲧⲉ ϯϫⲟⲙⲕ the sanctuary is opened which is covered by a black veil. The priest says the Thanksgivings prayer and offers the incense. They (the cantors) say ⲁⲙⲱⲓⲛⲓ ⲙⲁⲣⲉⲛⲟⲩⲱϣⲧ[149] and the Psalm 50 and we (the priests) incense the people without kissing and we read the ⲛⲓⲑⲩⲥⲓⲁ ⲛⲓⲡⲣⲟⲥ[150] and a chapter from the Praxis[151] with its own tune,[152] and we read the prophecy of Isaiah with the known tune after the Praxis, the tune is called the great Trisagion. We sing the Psalm in Idribi or the tune of burial and we read the Gospel in the tune of sadness. We finish the prayer normally with the sermon, Tarh, ⲧⲱⲃϩ= and Kyrie Eleyson.

In the sext, we prepare and distribute the *qorban* as a remembrance of the New Passover which our Lord -to whom is the Glory- prelude this day and then He abolished the Passover of the unleavened bread.[153]

We pray the prayer of tierce, sext and none and we fill the Basin with water. This is a built tank in the middle of the Church. The clergymen assemble around it, then we start with the prayer of Thanksgiving, Psalm 50, and a Chapter from the Law which begins with= ⲫϯ ⲇⲉ ⲟⲩⲱⲛϩ ⲛⲁⲃⲣⲁⲁⲙ "God appeared to Abraham" and ends with= ⲡⲓⲑⲙⲏⲓ ⲙ̅ⲫⲣⲏϯ ⲙ̅ⲡⲓⲁⲥⲉⲃⲏⲥ "The right like the evil."

And, from the Law which begins with ϧⲉⲛ ⲡϫⲓⲛⲑⲣⲉ ⲡⲓⲥ̅ⲗ̅ "and when Israel went across" and ends with ϫⲉ ϧⲉⲛ ⲟⲩⲱⲟⲩ ⲅⲁⲣ ⲁϥϭⲓⲱⲟⲩ "For with glory, He was glorified."

And a Chapter from the book of Joshua son of Nun which begins with ⲓⲏⲥⲟⲩ ⲛⲉⲙ ⲡⲓⲗⲁⲟⲥ "Joshua and the people" and ends with= ⲉⲩⲣⲁϣⲓ ⲛⲟⲩϫⲁϫⲓ "And they destroyed their enemies."

149	Amoyni marenošt = come let us worship
150	Nithisia nipros= The sacrifices and the offerings
151	The Acts of the Apostles.
152	This means the tune of the Praxis of the Maundy Thursday.
153	This rite is not actually observed.

From Isaiah the prophet which begins with= ϧⲉⲛ ⲡⲓⲉϩⲟⲟⲩ ⲉⲧⲉⲙⲙⲁⲩ "In this day" and ends with= ⲛⲉⲙ ⲛⲉⲛϣⲏⲣⲓ ⲛⲥⲓⲟⲛ "and the sons of Zion."

From Ezekiel the Prophet which begins with ⲛⲁⲓ ⲛⲉ ⲉⲧⲁϥϫⲱ ⲙⲙⲟⲥ "These what Lord said" and ends with= ⲉⲃⲟⲗϧⲉⲛ ⲛⲉⲧⲉⲛⲁⲛⲟⲙⲓⲁ "from all yours sins."

And also from Ezekiel the Prophet which begins with= ⲟⲩⲟϩ ⲁϥⲟⲗⲧ ⲉϧⲟⲩⲛ "And then I had been transported to" and ends with= ⲟⲩⲟϩ ⲥⲉⲛⲁⲱⲛϧ=± and they will live."[154]

The *Apostolos*[155] Timothy I, which begins with= ⲉⲛϩⲟⲧ ⲛϫⲉ ⲡⲥⲁϫⲓ "The word is true" and ends with=ϩⲱⲃ ⲛⲓⲃⲉⲛ ⲉⲑⲛⲁⲛⲉⲩ= "In every good action". Then they say Agios and the prayer of the Gospel and after that the psalm response which begins with ⲉⲕⲉⲛⲟⲩϫϧ ⲉϫⲱⲓ ⲙⲡⲉⲕϣⲉⲛϩⲩⲥⲟⲡⲟⲛ "Take hyssop and sprinkle me, that I may be clean"

The Gospel that is read is from John, which begins with= ⲁϫⲉⲛ ⲡϣⲁⲓ ⲇⲉ ⲛⲧⲉ ⲡⲓⲡⲁⲥⲭⲁ "Before the feast of the Passover" and ends with ⲉϣⲱⲡ ⲁⲣⲉⲧⲉⲛϣⲁⲛⲁⲓⲧⲟⲩ= "if you did so"

The Gospel is sung according to the annual tune and when the reader reaches the word "he tied the towel round him. Then he poured water into basin", the priest ties a towel around himself and pours water in the *Basin* in the form of the Cross three times. And the priest says during the interpretation[156] of the Gospel[157]:ⲡⲓⲧⲉϥⲟⲩⲱⲛϩⲏⲧ=until the end=± ϧⲉⲛ ⲣ̄ ⲛⲉⲙ ⲝ̄ ⲛⲉⲙ ⲗ̄"[158]

And after the interpretation; the priest raises up the Cross and the people say ten times Kyrie Eleyson with the great tune.

---

154   Note that the actual rite also adds readings from Proverbs 9:1-11. Isaiah 55:1-13. Exodus 36:25-28, in addition to a Sermon. We can conclude that the readings are actually the replica of those of the fourteenth century.
155   In the manuscript, it means the Pauline Epistle.
156   It means the translation into Arabic.
157   During the reading of the Arabic text.
158   khen še nem se nem map = in 100, 60 and 30)

And then, they say the seven litanies and their supplication concerning the *Basin*. Their number is 16:

1. Who tied himself by a towel.

2. Who by his loving for mankind.

3. Who he prepared for us the way of life.

4. Christ our God.

5. Who bears light like a garment.

6. Misere nobis; Domine, secundum magnam misericordiam tuam.

7. Lord our God the Almighty.

8. Who gathered waters.

9. Who put the waters in his hand and the sky in his palm.

10. Who did the sources to become rivers.

11. And who truly gives.

12. Irrigate harvest and multiply their fruits.

13. Make rejoice the surface of the Earth.

14. Let the Land of Egypt rejoices

15. Rescue your people.

16. Give security to the king.[159]

And after every supplication they say Kyrie Eleyson . And after these, the priest concludes the supplication and the people say Kyrie Eleyson 100 times.

Following, three prayers are said: for the peace, the fathers, and the congregations and the Creed. The deacon says; ⲡⲣⲟⲥⲫⲉⲣⲓⲛ[160]= to which the priest replies ⲟ ⲕ̅ⲥ̅[161]= and signs the water while saying ⲁⲝⲓⲟⲛ ⲕⲉ ⲇⲓⲕⲉⲟⲛ ⲅ̅[162] (three times) and a prayer which begins with: ⲫⲛⲏⲃ ⲡ̅ⲟ̅ⲥ̅ ⲡⲉⲛⲥⲱ̅ⲣ̅.[163] And

---

159 Exactly as the actual rite.
160 prosferin = offer
161 O kyrios = The Lord
162 Axion kai dhikeon = might and worthy
163 Fneeb pchois pensoter = Lord God our Saviour. I did not find this prayer

CHAPTER X: *The Fourteenth Century* **87**

the deacon replies:=ι καθημενη[164]. And another prayer. the deacon says: Look towards the East. And they[165] say: ⲁⲅⲓⲟⲥ ⲁⲅⲓⲟⲥ[166]. And a prayer[167] and Our Father, and the priest says the absolution of the Son. The deacon says: ⲙⲉⲧⲁ ⲫⲟⲃⲟⲩ.[168] And the priest blesses the water with the cross. And he says: "One is the Holy Father" and the psalm 150 according to the tradition. The priest washes the feet and the hands of the people, greeting them (one by one)' Let God make you live'. And the people sing this hymn in the Batos tune like= ⲡⲓⲕⲉⲃⲉⲣⲛⲓⲧⲏⲥK[169] The beginning is ⲡⲉⲛⲟ̄ⲥ̄ ⲁϥⲭⲱ ⲛⲛⲉϥϩⲱⲃⲥ[170] and the number of santzas is six. They are sung in the tune of the ⲗⲱⲃϣ of the Theotokia of Thursday which is ⲡⲓⲟⲩⲁⲓ ⲉⲃⲟⲗϧⲉⲛ ϯⲧⲣⲓⲁⲥ[171] and according to the melody of sadness because this day is the commemoration of the New Passover and the future joy, which washes our sins and the humiliation of the Lord of Glory for the salvation of mankind.

And after that a prayer of Thanksgivings on the *Basin* which begins with ⲫϯ ⲡⲓⲡⲁⲛⲧⲟⲕⲣⲁⲧⲱⲣ[172],the deacon says "Pray" and the priest concludes the prayer. The clergy enter to the sanctuary for the *Prothesis*[173] of the qorban

The foot washing is not placed before the offering because Our Lord washed the feet of His disciples before He broke

---

in the actual rite which starts by ϥⲉⲙⲡϣⲁ.

164   I kathemani =Who are seated stand up.
165   The congregation, the cantors...
166   Agios Agios = Holy, Holy
167   I do not know what Ibn Kabar means by this prayer. The actual rite contains another 11 supplications ending with Amen and then 4 other supplications not mentioned at all in Ibn Kabar. We may ask ourselves were these prayers known during the time of Ibn Kabar or they had been added later? Or whether these prayers are from two different local traditions amalgamated together.
168   Meta phobo theou = In the fear of God
169   This is the first word of the doxology of Severus of Antioch showing the annual tune.
170   our Saviour put down his clothes.
171   The One from the Trinity.
172   Lord God the Almighty.
173   offering.

the bread, blessed it, and gave it to His disciples, following which the sacred Chalice. These are the holy words of the Gospels. In fact, the Gospels of Matthew, Mark and Luke did not mention the foot washing but only the sharing of the bread and the Chalice. John mentioned the foot washing without mentioning neither the bread nor the Chalice but noted that Lord, having washed their feet, returned back to table. And hence, the order of the event can be inferred as such. For the *proemium*[174] of the Mass, they read the Paulos[175] according to the annual tune and according to the melody of sadness. -There are some people who used to read all the text according to the annual tune and others according to the melody of sadness.

Neither the Catholicon nor the Praxis are read. They used to say that they were read formerly, and I found a Manuscript of the Passover which contains a lesson of the Catholicon from the Epistle of Peter chapter 3[176] which begins with "What credit is there in fortitude when you have done wrong and are beaten for it" and ends with "but now you have turned towards the Shepherd and Guardian of your souls."[177]

The Praxis is already read during the morning office, and we add, and He was counted with the twelve.[178]

Most of the people read only the Paulos and nothing more.

And after that, the Trisagion, the Psalm and Gospel are sung according to the annual tune. The Gospel is from the 32° section[179] of Matthew.[180] They did not kiss the Gospel in this

---

174   The beginning
175   Pauline Epistle
176   This means that in the XIV century this lesson was not observed for a long time.
177   I Peter 2:20-25.
178   The Praxis of the prayer of the Basin.
179   There were ancient different sections for the Gospels not corresponding to what is used nowadays.
180   According to the editor of the text of Ibn Kabar, this is an error, and it should be corrected as the Gospel of John.

CHAPTER X: *The Fourteenth Century*

day because of the kiss of Judas. They did not say the prayer of peace which is the Aspasmos[181], and there is no mutual kiss between the people nor did they say the diptych of the dead.

When the Priest says=ⲁⲣⲓⲫⲙⲉⲩⲓ ⲡ̅ⲟ̅ⲥ̅ ⲛⲛⲏⲉⲧⲁⲩⲓⲛⲓ ⲛⲁⲕ ⲉⲃⲟⲩⲛ ⲛⲉⲙ ⲛⲏⲉⲧⲁⲩⲉⲛⲟⲩ the people say ⲱⲥⲡⲉⲣ ⲓⲛ.[182] The priest continues and says ϩⲓⲛⲁ ⲛⲉⲙ ⲃⲉⲛ[183] And he finishes the Mass with the communion of the people. They did not say psalm 150. And there is no dismissal but a lesson from the prophecy of Isaiah the prophet and the psalm and the Gospel of John with the melody of sadness.

And the first hour of the night they read the lessons of the Paraclete from the Gospel of John which are four in number. These readings are reserved for the priests according to their ranks. For the other hours of the nights, they read four lessons from the Holy Gospel, one per Gospel, in order to get a mutual witness.

Mention of the rite of the Good Friday

They say the prayer of the first hour according to the rite of the Passover. They read four lessons from the four Gospels and the prophecies and the sermons which are arranged for this hour.

When it is time of the tierce, they hang veils on the Higab[184] and the doors of the sanctuary. They hang seven censers on the door of the ⲥⲕⲏⲛⲏ.[185]= They put the icon of the glorified crucifixion out of the ⲥⲕⲏⲛⲏ=because Jesus had been crucified out of the city. They place next to the icon some aromatic

---

181   Hymn during exchanging the kiss of peace, this is a Greek word meaning greeting.
182   arifmevi pchois enitavini nak ekhoun nem nietavenou = remember O Lord those who offered and what they offered, as it was...
183   hina nem khen = so with
184   Which is the screen, (called iconostasis from the Byzantine rite).
185   This is a Greek word meaning the stage of the theatre which is used in English as "scene" That means not only the dome but also what is inside the sanctuary.

herbs. And they read the prophecies, Gospels, sermons, Tarh and they conclude.

During the Sext after the reading of the prophecies, they sing ⲐⲰⲔ ⲦⲈ ϮϪⲞⲘ ⲚⲈⲘ ⲠⲒⲰⲞⲨ.= They prepare the censers, and the priests offer incense to the icon of crucifixion according to their ranks. They read the Apostolos[186] with the melody of sadness. This text is from the Epistle to Galatians which begins with "I should not boast of anything but the Cross of our Lord Jesus Christ."[187] And when it is finish the reader says ⲠϨⲘⲞⲦ ⲄⲀⲢ ⲚⲈⲘⲰⲦⲈⲚ[188] - some people used to say this with two melodies one of the sadness and the normal one, and this practice is wrong. And after that, they say ⲀⲄⲒⲞⲤ ⲆⲈ ⲎⲘⲀⲤ and agios of the middle three times with the great tune,[189] which is mirrored within the Greeks.[190] And they say the stanza of the sext as in the Horologion (Agpeya). They sing the psalm and they read the Gospels, the sermons and the tarh which are tailored to that hour. They conclude and the people sit down and sing the Middle ⲀⲄⲒⲞⲤ briefly.[191]

And then the faithfulness (confession) of the thief in Greek and in Arabic. And after every stanza, the cantors answer the reader in two choirs one in Coptic and the other in Greek, the Greek is= ⲘⲚⲎⲤ ⲐⲨⲦⲒ= and the Coptic is= ⲀⲢⲒⲠⲀⲘⲈⲨⲒ Ⲱ ⲠⲀ.[192] And when the confession is finished, they sing the hymn of the right Thief which is ⲰⲞⲨⲚⲒⲀⲦⲔ ⲚⲐⲞⲔ Ⲱ ⲆⲒⲘⲀⲤ ⲠⲒⲤⲞⲚⲒ ⲠⲀⲢⲀ ⲞⲨⲞⲚ,= "Blessed are you Demas the thief more than anybody" And they sing the Paralex which is==.[193] The

---

186   The Pauline Epistle
187   Galat. 6:14.
188   pihmot ghar nemoten = for the grace be with you
189   Which is « who was crucified for us."
190   It is amazing that Ibn Kabar here assumed that the Greeks (the byzantine) have this stanza and as we saw in the previous chapter that many riots took place during the reign of Anastasius for this text "who was crucified for us."
191   As they are several Agios, one after the Pauline Epistle, another after O Only Begotten, hence, Ibn Kabar considers this as a middle agios
192   Remember me O Lord…
193   Asšopi etaviši mpensoter = It happens that when they crucified our Saviour.

CHAPTER X: *The Fourteenth Century*   91

candles and lamps are extinguished during this hour till the none as it is attested in the Holy Gospel.[194]

A homily of Anba James, Bishop of Sarûg, on the confession of the thief and his entrance to the Paradise with the Lord and other homilies and sermons explaining the sections of the Gospels of the Crucifixion are read if there is enough time.

Then they read the none. They say some of the ninth hour litanies in the Agpeya[195] in the usual tune before reading the psalms.

For the eleventh hour, there is a tradition that their prophecies and their Gospels are to be read by the eldest deacons so the Gospel of John (XIX:31-37) is read by the archdeacon.

When they finish, they pray the twelfth hour. The whole readings of this hour are for the priest and the Gospel of John (XIX:38-42) is reserved for the patriarch- if he is present- or the bishop of the diocese, or the archdeacon.. The custom in the Church of al-Muallaqah in Misr (Old-Cairo), is that the patriarch reads over the ⲕⲁⲑⲉⲇⲣⲁ[196],And that the ⲧⲱⲃϩ is read. Then they raise the cross and they say Kyrie Eleison 400 times: 100 towards the East, 100 towards the west, 100 towards the north and 100 towards the south using the Passover tune. When it is finished the clergy and the people turn towards the east twelve Kyrie Eleyson are sung in the great melody of the annual tune. . They sing after that the canon of the cross which is ϩⲓⲧⲉⲛ ⲡⲉⲕⲥⲧⲁⲩⲣⲟⲥ[197] could also sing=ⲁⲩϯϥⲧ ⲛⲁⲕ ⲱ ⲡⲓⲥⲧⲁⲩⲣⲟⲥ[198] Finally the blessing is said.

And the patriarch or the highest ranking priest reads the first three psalms and the people leave the church.

194	"And there was darkness over all the land…"
195	i.e. Troparia cf. p. XXX
196	This word means the seat of the Patriarch.
197	Hiten pekstavros = through Your Cross.
198	avtift nak o pistavros = they nailed You O Cross.

Then, the patriarch puts the cross in a piece of cloth symbolizing the burial of the body of our Lord with lots of aromatic spices, plants, and roses symbolizing the perfumes of the burial.

Then they read the whole book of psalms starting with the priests and then the deacons. When they reach psalm 148, the archpriest or the highest ranking priest reads the last three psalms and the patriarch or the bishop reads psalm 151 in Coptic and the archdeacon translates it in Arabic. Then they put the book of psalms in a piece of silk and the deacon raises it to his head. they go around the church with candles and singing Kyrie Eleyson. with the Passover tune. It is better to sing ⲘⲀⲢⲈⲚⲞⲨⲰⲚϨ until they return back to the place where is the great priest[199] and they read the canticles one after the other.

In Upper Egypt, they are all read by the archdeacon. In the churches of Misr (Old Cairo) the archdeacon translates them into Arabic.

And when the reader arrives to the canticles of Moses (Exodus XV) and reads ⲬⲈ ⲘⲀⲢⲈⲚϨⲰⲤ ⲈⲠⲞ̄Ⲥ̄[200] then the singers sing ⲬⲈ ϦⲈⲚ ⲞⲨⲰⲞⲨ[201] and after they sing= ⲈⲚ ⲞⲨϢⲰⲦ ⲀϤϢⲰⲦ ⲚⲬⲈ ⲠⲒⲘⲰⲞⲨ[202] as usual.

Then they read the story of the three young men.

The rite of the Passover in the Monastery of Saint Abû Macarius

Ibn Saba'

We owe the other description to another Coptic writer called Yûhanna Ibn Abî Zakariah Ibn al Saba'. He is the author of a book called *Precious Pearl in the Ecclesiastic Science,*[203] but we do not know anything about the

---

199	As the priest remained in his seat and not going around the church with them
200	Marenhos epchois = let us praise the Lord.
201	Je khen ouoou = for with glory.
202	Khen oušot afšot = with the split:
203	Mistrih, 1966, p. 322-342.

life of the author except that he lived in the XIV century. His description is brief - not like Ibn Kabar who gave the rite in the Monastery of Shahran, the Muallaquah Church, the rite in Upper Egypt and in the Monastery of Saint Macarius- but useful.

The Palm Sunday

After the Epiphany is the feast of the Palm Sunday commemorating the entry of Lord Christ into Jerusalem on a donkey.

After the ninth hour of the Palm Sunday, the whole Christian congregation return, men, women, servants, maidservants, return to the church, the reason of the funeral service for the Passion Week is consecrated to Christ for his passions and his choice to Cross with the grief of Christ there is no grief.

The funeral is for everyone as usual, starting with the offering of incense, while the congregation prays the sorrow tunes of the funeral service. Then, the Pauline Epistle which begins with I inform you my brethren... and the Gospel the absolutions as usual. Lord have mercy 100 times and after that the mimar and the congregation welcomes the Pascha with the eleventh hour of Sunday.

Mention of the Passion week and what Pascha should have.

When it is the sunset of the Palm Sunday, they (the congregation) receive the Passion Week.

The prayer starts with Doxa Patri[204] our Father who art in heaven, Thok te tigom 12times in every hour and the prophecies included in the book of Pascha, in each hour, the Psalm using the Idribi tune the explanation for each hours the litanies (tobhat) and the patriarch or the high priest recites alone Fnuti nai nan.[205] Upon its end, the whole congregation prays Kyrie Eleyson with the tune of the Passion Week.

The priests say the blessing which ends may the blessing of the passion of Christ our Saviour...

---
204   Glory be to the Father.
205   Lord have mercy upon us.

The mention of Thursday the New Convent and the basin and the Mass.

When it is the Thursday of the slaughtering of the real lamb, the doors of the sanctuary open as the custom and the high priest advances and washes his feet. He enters to the sanctuary and offers the incense as usual. Afterwards; "come and worship Christ our God" three times and the psalm 50 and the Praxis (the Acts) with the tune of the Maundy Thursday in Coptic and Arabic. The three agios, the first and the second for the Nativity and the third for the crucifixion, the mention of resurrection is not mentioned on this day. (The priest) he recites the litany of the Gospel and offers the incense without kissing the Gospel because of the kiss of Judah.

Then, the psalms are read Idribi and the Gospel and the Tarh and they continue like the hours of the Pascha. They continue the third, sixth and ninth hours as usual.

The high priest advances to the basin and reads what is included in the book of the Lakkan and after the rite of basin the high priest advance as washes the feet of the congregation one by one as the example of Christ.

The second priest[206] starts the service of the mass, without the prayer of reconciliation because of the kiss of Judah and without the prayers for the dead…

Faraj Allah Al-Akhmimi

Farraj Allah al-Akhmimi is the compiler of a collection of church canons. Nothing is known about him, but he was originally from Akhmim but he lived for at least part of his life in Syria around the first quarter of the fourteenth century. He seems to be deacon.

His work survives in one manuscript in Paris Arabic 250.

This author expresses that the fasting for the Holy Week should only be with water and salt, and the Good Friday and Saturday without eating. Moreover, the women should not wear any jewelry.[207]

---

206 Lit. "Who is less than him."
207 Botros al-Baramusi, 2022, p.362-363.

CHAPTER XI

THE FIFTEENTH CENTURY

Litany Of The Evening

Although it is hard to know the exact date of a Coptic liturgical prayer, we may assume that this prayer was composed later than the XIV century. In fact Ibn Kabar did not include it in his encyclopedia.

In one of this litany, we read " نجينا من الغلاء والوباء والجلاء وسيف الاعداء"

"Save us from inflation, the plague, exile and the sword of the enemies."

We can say that this litany was written during the Mamluk period, perhaps during the reign of al-Zahir Baibars or later when Egypt was stricken by the Black death and the governor wanted to banish Copts from Egypt. In addition, the water level of the Nile did not increase in these years which cause famine in Egypt.

The studies of the German scholar Baumstark shows clearly that author of this Litany had excellent knowledge of the early liturgies. He underlined many Arabic expressions in this text, which occur in the Greek Liturgy of St. Mark attributed to St. Cyril.[208] Baumstark also mentions that the beginning of the Litany of the Lent and Holy Week "ⲕⲗⲓⲛⲱⲙⲉⲛ ⲧⲁ

---

208   Baumstark & Heffening, 1941, p. 74-100.

ⲅⲟⲛⲁⲧⲁ ⲁⲛⲁⲥⲧⲱⲙⲉⲛ ⲕⲁⲓⲛⲱⲙⲉⲛ ⲧⲁ ⲅⲟⲛⲁⲧⲁ" is from the first centuries from the time of the popes St. Cyprian and St. Cornelius.[209]

Macrizi's Description

Macrizi is a Muslim historian from the XV century. He compiled his chronicles from various sources some of them are Coptic, in addition to that, he added what he knew. This is what he wrote about the Coptic Passover.[210]

The Palm Sunday

> The feast of Olive known also to them as the feast of Hosanna (Shaanin) which means the praising. It is the seventh Sunday of their lent and their tradition in the Feast of Shaanin is to go out of the church with palms saying that this is the day in which Christ entered Jerusalem (al-Qods) and Zion on a donkey. He (Christ) was followed by people who sang. Christ ordered them to do good deeds and instructed them against doing evil.. In this feast, the Christians in Misr (Old Cairo) used to decorate their Churches. It happened on the last day of Rajjab 378 A.H. (989 A.D), the feast of Shaanin (Hosanna), Hakim Bi-Amar alla Abû Ali Mansûr ibn al Aziz Bi-allah forbad Christians from decorating their Churches and taking the palms as their custom.[211]

Maundy Thursday

> Three days before the Passover the Christians used to celebrate the Maundy Thursday and according to their customs, they used to fill a basin and prayed on it before washing the feet of all Christians. They replicate what Christ did with his disciples on that day in order to teach them humility and He got their oath to be humble towards each other. The common people in Misr (Old Cairo) called this day the Thursday of Lentils, because Christians cooked lentils, and offered to

---

209 Baumstark, 1958, p. 77-78.
210 Griveau, 1915, p. 318.
211 We may notice that the procession of the palms used to be around the city.

CHAPTER XI: *The Fifteenth Century*

each other and to Muslims a variety of fish with lentil soup. However, this custom has been abolished.

Saturday of Joy

This is one day before the Passover and they pretend that light comes out of the tomb of Christ in the Church of the Resurrection in Jerusalem (al-Qods) and then they light the lanterns of the Church. But after the investigation of trusted people, they concluded that this charade made for good business for the Christians.[212]

The Passover (the Easter)[213]

This is the great feast for them, and they pretend that the Christ -peace be on him- was killed by crucifixion because of agitated Jews.

The Canon Of The Twelfth Hour Of The Good Friday[214]

As we have previously seen, the Trisagion "Holy God! Holy Mighty! Holy Immortal!" is sung in every ceremony of the Coptic Church. The Coptic Church adds: "Who had been crucified, Have mercy upon us" which, according to a legend, comes from a hymn sung by Nicodemus and Joseph of Arimathea at the Lord's entombment.[215] In this chapter, we will examine the mention of Joseph of Arimathea and Nicodemus in the medieval books in order to detect the origin of this legend.

We will give hereafter two quotations of this legend:

The book of the order of the Holy Week mentions in the canon[216] *of the*

---

212 This paragraph Macrizi says that the light is fake, we have to put in mind that he was a Muslim fanatic and his point of view is obviously against Christianity.

213 The terms of Macrizi are confused as he is reflecting his Islamic point of view.

214 For more details cf. Youhanna Nessim Youssef, 2004, p. 147-159.

215 Moftah, Robertson, Roy, Toth, 1991, p. **1715a-1747b.**

216 For this word, cf. Graf, 1954, p. 87:2. Burmester gave three definitions to

twelfth hour:

ⲁⲩⲓ ⲛϫⲉ ⲛⲓⲇⲓⲕⲉⲟⲥ ⲓⲱⲥⲏⲫ ⲛⲉⲙ ⲛⲓⲕⲟⲇⲏⲙⲟⲥ ⲁⲩϭⲓ ⲛⲧⲥⲁⲣⲝ ⲛⲧⲉ ⲡⲭ̅ⲥ̅ ⲁⲩϯ ⲙⲡⲓⲥⲟϫⲉⲛ ⲉϩⲣⲏⲓ ⲉϫⲱϥ ⲁⲩⲕⲟⲥϥ ⲁⲩⲭⲁϥ ϧⲉⲛ ⲟⲩⲙϩⲁⲩ ⲉⲩϩⲱⲥ ⲉⲣⲟϥ ⲉⲩϫⲱ ⲙⲙⲟⲥ ϫⲉ ⲁⲅⲓⲟⲥ ⲟ ⲑⲉⲟⲥ ⲁⲅⲓⲟⲥ ⲓⲥⲭⲩⲣⲟⲥ ⲁⲅⲓⲟⲥ ⲁⲑⲁⲛⲁⲧⲟⲥ ⲟ ⲥⲧⲁⲩⲣⲱⲑⲉⲓⲥ ⲇⲏⲙⲁⲥ ⲉⲗⲉⲏⲥⲟⲛ ⲏⲙⲁⲥ

ⲁⲛⲟⲛ ϩⲱⲛ ⲙⲁⲣⲉⲛⲟⲩⲱϣⲧ ⲙⲙⲟϥ ⲉⲛⲱϣ ⲉⲃⲟⲗ ⲉⲛϫⲱ ⲙⲙⲟⲥ ϫⲉ ⲛⲁⲓ ⲛⲁⲛ ⲫⲛⲟⲩϯ ⲡⲉⲛⲥⲱⲧⲏⲣ ⲫⲏⲉⲧⲁⲩⲁϣϥ ⲉⲡⲓⲥⲧⲁⲩⲣⲟⲥ ⲉⲕⲉϧⲟⲙϧⲉⲙ ⲙⲡⲥⲁⲧⲁⲛⲁⲥ ⲥⲁⲡⲉⲥⲏⲧ ⲛⲛⲉⲛϭⲁⲗⲁⲩϫ

The righteous Joseph and Nicodemus came and took away Christ's Body and placed ointment on Him, wrapped Him and placed Him in a tomb, <u>praising Him, and saying: "Holy God, Holy mighty, Holy immortal, Who was crucified for us, have mercy upon us.</u>

We also worship Him, crying and saying: "Have mercy upon us, O God, our Saviour, Who was crucified on the cross and crushed Satan under our feet."[217]

This hymn was published for the first time by Tuki in 1736[218]

The hymn clearly refers to the same tradition, i.e. Joseph and Nicodemus sung the hymn with the addition "Who was crucified for us have mercy upon us".

Ibn Kabar

Shams al-Riyasah abu al-Barakat called Ibn Kabar[219] mentioned that the canon of the twelfth hour is

ϩⲓⲧⲉⲛ ⲡⲉⲕⲥ̅ⲧ̅ⲥ̅   :ويقال قانون الصليب وهو هذا

---

this word:
An ecclesiastical decree or rule.
2- A type of hymn.
3- The Eucharistic Prayer including the Epiclesis.
Cf. Burmester, 1975, p. 322.

217　　Attallah Arsenius al-Muharraqi, 1970, p. 191-193.
218　　Tuki, 1736, p. 250-251.
219　　Cf supra.

CHAPTER XI: *The Fifteenth Century*

ⲁⲩϯϥⳬ ⲛⲁⲕ ⲱ ⲡⲉⲕⲧ︦ⲥ︦ وهذا ايضاً موافق وهو

²²⁰ وتقال البركة

And they sing the Canon of the Cross, which is thus, "By your Cross," and this also is suitable i.e: You had been nailed to the Cross"[221]

The Canon mentioned by Ibn Kabar, is not known in the actual liturgical books related to the Holy Week.[222]

We can say positively that Ibn Kabar did not know the tradition of the trisagion sung by Joseph and Nicodemus. In a chapter about the apostles, Ibn Kabar mentioned that Nicodemus was one of the great priests and he confessed Christ in front of the Apostles and endured persecution with them. After the apostles had gone away for preaching, he became one of the heads of the Church.[223]

Ibn Kabar mentioned that Joseph of **Arimathea**, is the one who asked for Christ's body, which he embalmed and buried in a tomb. He preached in the Galilea and the Decapolis and died at his home in Arimethea.[224]

Also Ibn Kabar mentioned Joseph of Arimathea and Nicodemus concerning the holy Chrism (Myron).[225]

The Manuscript Tradition Of The Holy Week

The manuscript tradition confirms the actual Canon of the Twelfth hour was composed after the fourteen/fifteenth century.

There is a detailed description in M. Cramer's study of the fourteenth century manuscript Copt 9 in the *National Library of Vienna*. This manuscript is from the monastery of Our Lady Baramus in Wadi Natrun. It is mentioned there[226]:

و بعد ذلك يتوجهوا الى فوق بالقونة الدفن ويكملوا بقراآة القانون كالعادة

---

220 Wadi, "2001, p. 233-322 especially p. 272. Mina foundation, p 156-157.
221 Villecourt 1925, p. 290.
222 Wadi, 2001, p. 312.
223 . This quotation is taken from the popular edition with the introduction by Samir Khalil, 1971, p. 86.
224 Samir Khalil, 1971, p. 86.
225 Cf. Infra
226 We keep the text as in the manuscript.

"And after that, they return back with the icon of the entombment and continue reading the canon according to the custom."[227]

However, it is hard to discern which 'canon' is referred to in the manuscript. The editor of the text refers to the edited text!

The Manuscript: 168 Hymn. 5, 192 Hymn 29 in the collection of the State and University library of Hamburg, originally from the monastery of Saint Macarius, which could be dated to the fourteenth century did not include this hymn.[228]

Another manuscript from the monastery of Saint Pishoy and now preserved in the Hamburg collection, which could be dated to the eighteenth century, did not include this hymn.[229]

The Turuhat

In the Tarh[230] of the twelfth hour of the Good Friday, we read:

> A rich man whose name was Joseph, he was a councilor, knowing the Law, came. A graceful, blessed, God-loving, man whose name is Nicodemus (came).
>
> This Joseph, also, he and his fathers, used to care for the bodies of the saints. He went to Pilate and asked for the body of the Word, the Unique Son of God... The righteous councilor received His Body (of Jesus) and he took care of it. He brought some white and pure dresses, as is worthy of the Son of God.
>
> Nicodemus brought about one hundred pounds of precious perfumes...[231]

---

227   Cramer, 1963, p. 118-128, Id., 1965, p. 90-115, Id., 1966, p. 72-130 and especially p. 94-95.
228   Störk, 1995, p. 349-350, 396-397.
229   Burmester, 1975, p. 255-256.
230   For the Turuhat cf. Burmester, 1937, p. 78-109, p. 505-549; Bishop Gregorius, 1991, p. 1106a-1109b.
231   Philotheus al-Maqari and Mikhail Girgis, 1914, p. 241-243. Attalah Arsenius al-Muharraqi, 1969, 251 -249p

CHAPTER XI: *The Fifteenth Century*

As we mentioned, the book of Turahat took its present shape in the thirteenth century.²³² It was received as a tradition by the early fourteenth century, and was included in the book of Ibn Kabar, even with some anomalies such as the Tarh of the Joyful Saturday²³³

Yuhanna Ibn Abi Zakaria Ibn Al-Siba'

The first Coptic author who refers to the same tradition is Yuhanna Ibn Abi Zakaria Ibn al-Siba'²³⁴ nothing is known about the author except that he may have lived in the fourteenth century. The oldest known manuscript dated A.M. 20 Tubah 1164/A.D. 1448, is housed in the Egyptian Public Library.²³⁵

ان يوسف ونيقوديموس بعد حنوط السيد له المجد وحمل الى القبر ليدفن فكان القبر مغارة كما شهد الانجيل انه قبراً جديداً لم يكن ترك فيه احد ولما انزلوه في القبر تحققنا موته مثل كل البشر وما كان في علمهم انه يقوم ثالث يوم كما في الكتب نعوه وندبوه عليه يا من كنا نرجوا انه عزا اسرائيل ومخلصه من بقى يعزينا وينجينا وهم باكين ظهر الملايكه وهم قايلين قدوس الله قدوس القوي قدوس الذي لا يموت وعندما قالوا الذي لا يموت والرب فتح عينيه في وجوههم اعطوه الملايكه هذه التسبحة ... فتحققوا ذلك انه لم يموت قهرا بل بارادته فقال يوسف ونيقوديمس يالذي صلب عنا ارحمتا

> That Joseph and Nicodemus, after the embalming of the Lord, to whom is due glory, was taken to the tomb to be buried. The tomb was a cave, as attested in the Gospel, that it was a new tomb in which nobody had been placed before. And when they descended Him in the tomb, they were sure of His death like all human beings, and they did not know that He shall rise on the third day according to the Scriptures. They mourned Him and lamented (saying): "O whom we hoped that He would be the consolation of Israel and its Saviour. Who is going to console and save us?". And while weeping,

---

232   Burmester, 1937, p. 235-254 especially p236-237.
233   Muyser1952, p. 175-184.
234   For this author cf. Aziz S. Atiya, 1991, p. 1272a-1272b
235   We respect here the spelling of the manuscript which may differ from the actual spelling.

the angels appeared saying: "Holy God, Holy mighty, Holy immortal." And when they (the angels) said: "immortal,", the Lord opened His eyes[236] looking directly at them (Joseph and Nicodemus). They became sure that He did not die against His will but by His own will, then Joseph and Nicodemus said: "O who was crucified for us, have mercy upon us."[237]

We find here that the tradition quoted by Ibn al-Siba' is more developed than what we find in the Coptic hymn. He noticed the apparition of the Angels singing: "Holy God…" and then Joseph and Nicodemus added: "Who had been crucified for us save us."

However the late manuscripts of Ibn Saba' talking about the Holy week did not mention the actual Canon of the Holy week.[238]

وعند انتهى ذلك يرتل الشعب كيرياليصون وهم نازلين من الانبل الى حين يدوروا الهيكل بالقون والصلبان وغيره ثلاثة دورات ثم يقف حامل ايقونة الصلبوت قدام باب الهيكل ووجهه نحو الغرب ويرتل الشعب بقانون الصليبوت

"And when it is finished, the congregation sing: Lord Have Mercy while descending from the sanctuary, they turn three times around the altar holding icons, crosses etc. The carrier of the icon of crucifixion will stand in front of door of the sanctuary facing to the west and the congregation sing the **Canon of the Crucifixion.**"[239]

R Mouwad, drew my attention to the parallel between the eleventh century Syrian writer Yahya Ibn Garir[240] in his *Muršid* and the Maronite writer Thomas of Kfartab.[241] He mentioned that the origin of the story of Joseph of Arimathea and Nicodemus singing the addition "who was

---

236   This is the text of Ibn Saba but theologically speaking, Jesus suffered death like any human being. He was not acting or pretending to die. Hence, the resurrection became the great mystery of Christianity.

237   Mistrih, 1966, p. 202-203 (text), p.499 (translation).

238   We keep the text as in the Manuscript.

239   Mistrih, 1966, p. 341.

240   It seems that Ibn Kabar did not have a direct knowledge of the works this author. He put him among the Nestorians. Cf. Samir Khalil,, 1971, p. 301.

241   . Mouawad, "2003, p. 537-550.

crucified for us, save us;" is a Syrian one mentioned in the ninth century by Moses Bar Kepha in his commentary on the liturgy.[242]

The hymn of the holy Week does not mention the Seraphim who were mentioned by Moses Bar Kepha but it highlights the role of the faithful in singing the same.

Conclusion

Since J.M. Fiey had already proved that there were contacts and exchanges between Copts and Syrians,[243] it is hence possible to conclude that this Coptic tradition was taken from the Syriac parallel. It was introduced for the first time by the end of the thirteenth century. We can follow the steps of this tradition:

- In the sixth century (AD 518) Severus of Antioch delivered his last Cathedral homily on the Trisagion[244] defending the addition of "Who had been crucified for us." He did not mention the story of Jesus opening his eyes although this would be a good argument for using this epression.
- In the ninth century, the legend of Joseph and Nicodemus was introduced for the first time by Thomas Bar Képha. This means that this tradition existed before the ninth century.
- In the eleventh century, a Syriac Orthodox author Yahya Ibn Garir introduced the legend for the first time in Arabic.
- The author of the Tarh of the twelfth hour of the Good Friday (Thirteenth century?) did not know this tradition.
- Ibn Kabar (fourteenth century) did not mention this tradition neither while talking about Joseph and Nicodemus nor while talking about the canon of the twelfth hour of Good Friday. He did not even know that Yahya Ibn Garir (who mentioned this tradition) was Syrian Orthodox.
- The first Coptic author who mentioned this tradition is Ibn al-Siba'[245] (thirteenth-fourteenth centuries?) and as expected he did

---

242   Mouawad, "2003, p. 546-547.
243   Fiey, 1972-1973, p. 295-366
244   Brière, 1961, p. 247-249
245   Nothing is known about this author or his education, we believe that this

not mention the Syrian rite despite having had access to the Arabic version of Ibn Garir.
- Later, (between the fourteenth and the seventeenth centuries) this tradition had been introduced in the canon of the twelfth hour of the Holy Week, replacing two other canons mentioned by Ibn Kabar.
- In the 1736 AD, R. Tukhi published, for the first time, the Canon of the twelfth hour (reflecting this tradition) together with the other Canons mentioned by Ibn Kabar.
- In early twentieth century, the Coptic Orthodox editions of the order of the Holy Week and the Diaconal[246] included the canon of the twelfth hour only reflecting Joseph and Nicodemus' tradition of the Trisagion.
- By the end of the Twentieth century, it became as ***a legend received*** and accepted even by scholars (see Coptic Encyclopedia)

The Description Of Qalqašandî[247]

Qalqašandi who is Šhab al-Dîn Aḥmed ibn Ahmed al-Qalqašandî was born in a village called Qalqašanda in Qalyabiyah province in the year 765 AH (1355AD). He studied in Alexandria and Cairo where he became famous in the Shafi' law.

He attracted the attention of the Mameluke palaces. He joined the Dîwan in the year 791AH. And he died in the year 821AH (1418 AD).

In the beginning of the ninth century of the Hijra the Qalqašandi wrote his book "morning time for night-blind in the art of literature"

This encyclopedia intended to help the secretary of the chancellery wherein he assembled all knowledge for a good scribe. He included a calendar of the religious feasts of the Muslims, Persians, Copts, Sabaens, and Jews.

For the Copts:
- 23 Baramhat   Feast of Lazarus

---

would be a positive contribution.
246   The book of the service and hymns for the deacons
247   Coquin, 1975, p. 387-411, especially p.399-400.

CHAPTER XI: *The Fifteenth Century*

- 24 Baramhat   Feast of the Palm
- 25 Baramhat   Feast of *al-Marsunah*
- 28 Baramhat   Washing feet
- 29 Baramhat   Friday of the Crucifixion.

The feast of Lazarus preceding immediately the Palm Sunday is the Saturday of Lazarus. The feast of *al-Marsunah* is enigmatic.

Al-Marsunah could be a disfigured Coptic/Greek word ⲙⲁⲛⲥⲁⲕⲏ "the place fig tree." As we saw the holy Monday is the commemoration of the curse of fig-tree by Jesus-Christ.

We can also deduce that the date this was written was in the year 1407AD.

CHAPTER XII
THE SEVENTEENTH CENTURY

The author was a priest, ordained at the age of 26 years for the patriarchal church of the Virgin Mary, in Harit Zuweila in the time of the patriarch John of Mallawî (1619 - 1634 AD)

Whilst the author wrote the text in Coptic, it is apparent from many features that the author's mother tongue (ie. the language he thought in) was Arabic.

The author narrates a tradition that the Holy Week Lectionary was compiled by the Patriarch Gabriel Ibn Turaik (1131-1146 A.D.) with the help of the monks of the Monastery of St. Macarius. Further sections and also a number of short homilies or exhortations were afterwards added to the Lectionary by a certain Peter, bishop of Behnasa.

As it was demonstrated above that the origin of the Lectionary was earlier than this date, however the importance of the following text, is that it reflects that the attribution of Patriarch Gabriel Ibn Turaik, as mentioned above in this book, was known in the seventeenth century/ became accepted in the seventeenth century.

Here is the text:[248]

---

[248] We respect here the spelling of the manuscript even if it does not conform to the actual spelling.

Youhanna Nessim Youssef, "Psali of the Lectionary (revisited)", p. 143-174

ⲫⲕⲁⲛⲱⲛ ⲇⲉ ⲁⲥϣⲱⲡⲓ· ⲛ̀ⲁⲡⲟⲥⲧⲟⲗⲓⲕⲏ· ⲁϥⲥⲁϩⲛⲓ ⲉϫⲉⲛ ⲡⲓⲱϣ· ⲛ̀ϯⲡⲁⲗⲉⲁ ⲇⲉ ⲟⲛ	كان القانون الرسولي ·يامر بقراة العتيقة· باتفاق مع الحديث	The Apostolic canon had ordered the reading of the Old (Testament) also (with the New)
ⲭⲱⲥⲧⲁⲥⲓⲁ ⲛⲉⲙ ⲅⲉⲛⲉⲁ· ϧⲉⲛ ϯⲁⲃⲇⲱⲙⲁⲥ· ⲛ̀ⲛⲓⲙⲕⲁⲩϩ ⲛ̀ⲟⲩϫⲁⲓ· ⲛ̀ⲧⲉ ⲓⲏ̅ⲥ̅ ⲥⲱⲧⲏⲣⲁⲥ	في ستة الالام المحيية الذي ليسوع المخلص	In the six days of the passion week of salvation of Jesus, the Saviour
ⲯⲁⲗⲧⲏⲣⲓⲟⲛ ⲙ̀ⲡⲁⲓϫⲱⲙ· ⲡϣⲏⲣⲓ ⲛ̀ⲑⲟⲩⲣⲁⲓⲕ ⲡⲉⲛⲓⲱⲧ ⲁⲃⲃⲁ ⲅⲁⲃⲣⲓⲏⲗ· ⲟ̅ ⲙ̀ⲡⲁⲧⲣⲓⲁⲣⲭⲏⲥ	مرتب هذا المصحف · ابن تريك· الاب انبا غربيال · السبعون من البطاركة	The organiser of this book the son of Turaik, Abba Gabriel the seventieth patriarch
ⲱⲥⲁⲩⲧⲟⲥ ⲁϥϣⲱⲡⲓ· ⲟⲩⲥⲁϧ ⲛⲉⲙ ⲟⲩⲉⲙⲓ· ⲁϥⲛⲁⲩ ⲉⲛⲓⲣⲱⲙⲓ· ⲉⲧϫⲉⲛ ⲛⲟⲩϩⲃⲏⲟⲩⲓ	وكان مغبوطا· معلما عاملا· فرأى الناس في اشغالهم	And also he was a master and knowledgeable man. He saw the people in their workplaces.
ϣⲁⲧⲉϥⲛⲁⲩ ⲉⲛⲓⲣⲱⲙⲓ· ϧⲉⲛ ⲡϣⲉⲙϣⲓ ⲛ̀ⲛⲓⲉⲝⲟⲩⲥⲓⲁ· ⲙ̀ⲙⲟⲛϣϫⲟⲙ ⲁⲩⲓ̀· ⲉⲡϫⲱⲕ ⲙ̀ⲡⲁⲥⲭⲁ	فلما رأى الناس بخدمتهم للسلاطين· مل يقدروا ياتوا ·لتكملت البسخة	When he saw the people in the service of the authorities were not able to come to the complete pascha
ϥⲑⲱⲟⲩϯ ⲛ̀ⲥⲁⲃⲉⲩ ⲛⲉⲙ ⲕⲁⲧϩⲏⲧ · ⲛⲉⲙ ⲡⲓⲙⲏϣ ⲙ̀ⲙⲟⲛⲁⲭⲟⲥ· ϧⲉⲛ ⲡⲓⲙⲟⲛⲁⲥⲧⲏⲣⲓⲟⲛ· ⲙ̀ⲙⲁⲕⲁⲣⲓⲁ ϥⲑⲟⲩⲏⲧ	فجمع حكما و فهما · ورهبان كثيرة· من دير ابو مقار الطوباني	He assembled the wise and the knowledgeable and many monks in the monastery of Macarius together
ϧⲉⲛ ϯⲅⲉⲛⲉⲁ ⲁⲩϭⲓ· ⲛⲉⲙ ϧⲉⲛ ϯⲡⲁⲗⲉⲁ· ⲟⲩⲟϩ ⲟⲩϫⲱⲙ ⲁⲩⲓⲣⲓ ⲁⲩⲙⲟⲩϯ 36 ⲙ̀ⲡⲓⲡⲁⲥⲭⲁ	واخذوا من الحديثة · والعتيقة وجعلوه كتابا · واسموه البسخة	They took from the New (Testament) and the Old and they made a book, they called it the Pascha

CHAPTER XII: *The Seventeenth Century*

ϩⲓⲛⲁ ⲁϥ̀ⲓⲣⲓ ⲙ̀ⲡⲓϣⲁⲓ· ⲕⲁⲧⲁⲥⲩⲛⲏⲑⲓⲁ· ϧⲉⲛ ⲟⲩⲑⲉⲗⲏⲗ ⲛⲉⲙ ⲟⲩⲥⲁⲓ· ϧⲉⲛ ⲡⲥⲉⲡⲓ ⲛ̀ⲛⲏⲉⲕⲕⲗⲏⲥⲓⲁ	لكي يعملوا العيد كالعادة. بهجة وتحليل. في ساير كنايس	In order to make the feast according to the custom with joy and beauty with the rest of the churches
Ⲭⲉ ⲙⲉⲛⲉⲛⲥⲁ ⲛⲁⲓ ⲁϥϣⲱⲡⲓ· ⲡⲉⲛⲓⲱⲧ ⲛ̀ⲇⲓⲕⲉⲟⲥ · ⲕⲁⲧⲁ ⲥⲁ ⲛ̀ⲣⲏϯ· ⲡⲉⲧⲣⲟⲥ ⲡⲓⲉⲡⲓⲥⲕⲟⲡⲟⲥ	ومن بعد هذا. كان الاب المكرم بكل الانواع. انبا بطرس الاسقف	For after these, it happened that our righteous, according to every aspect, father Peter the Bishop
ϭⲟ ⲛ̀ϩⲣⲏⲓ ⲛ̀ϩⲏⲧⲥ· ϯⲡⲟⲗⲓⲥ ⲝⲉⲣⲓⲕⲟⲩ· ⲁϥⲛⲁⲩ ⲉⲣⲟⲥ ⲛ̀ϩⲏⲧⲥ· ⲁϥϣⲫⲏⲣⲓ ⲉⲙⲁϣⲱ	مدينة البهنسا . اخذ ينظر فيها. متعجب جدا	of the city of Oxyrhynchus, looked at it (the pascha book) and he was extremely amazed
Ϯⲟⲩⲛⲟⲩ ⲇⲉ ⲁⲩⲑⲁⲙⲓⲟ ϩⲁⲛⲙⲏϣ ⲙ̀ⲡⲣⲟⲫⲏⲧⲓⲁ· ⲛⲉⲙ ϩⲁⲛⲉⲩⲁⲅⲅⲉⲗⲓⲟⲛ· ⲛ̀ⲁⲧⲥⲩⲙⲫⲱⲛⲓⲁ	الانهم مل يعملوا بل ساعة والا انجيل واحد. وهو تعجب لذلك	They made many prophecies and Gospels without harmony in one hour, and each hour was not structured similarly.
ϭⲓ ⲛ̀ⲛⲓϫⲱⲙ ⲛ̀ⲑⲟϥ· ⲛ̀ⲡⲉⲛⲡⲣⲟⲫⲏⲧⲏⲥ· ⲛⲉⲙ ⲡⲓⲉⲩⲁⲅⲅⲉⲗⲓⲟⲛ· ⲛⲉⲙ ϩⲁⲛⲕⲉⲑⲏⲕⲉⲥⲏⲥ	فاخذ هو كتاب الانبيا . والاجليين والعظات	He took the books of prophets and the Gospels and the exhortations
Ⲭⲉ ⲁⲩⲁⲣⲭⲏ ⲛ̀ⲧⲉ ⲛⲓ ⲁⲩⲥϧⲁ· ⲉⲃⲟⲗⲛ̀ϩⲏⲧⲟⲩ ⲧⲏⲣⲟⲩ· ⲛⲉⲙ ⲏⲥⲟⲩ ⲛ̀ⲧⲉ ⲥⲩⲣⲁⲭ· ⲛⲉⲙ ⲥⲟⲗⲟⲙⲟⲛ ⲡⲟⲩⲣⲟ	وابتدوا يكتبون. منهم كلمتم . ومن يشوع بن شيراخ . ومن سليمان الملك	They started and wrote them all; and from Jesus son of Sirach to the king Solomon
Ϩⲁⲟⲩⲛⲟⲩ ⲇⲉ ⲁϥϩⲁⲓϥ· ⲙ̀ⲫⲛⲉⲧⲥϣⲉ ⲉⲣⲟⲥ· ϣⲁⲧⲟⲩϣⲱⲡⲓ ⲧⲏⲣⲟⲩ· ⲉⲩϩⲩⲥⲟⲥ ⲛⲉⲙ ⲛⲟⲩⲉⲣⲏⲟⲩ	وعملوا لكل ساعة . ما يناسب لها. حتى صاروا كلهم متساويين	They added to each hour what was required till they made all the hours balanced and similar in structure.

ϧⲉⲛ ⲟⲩⲉϩⲟⲟⲩ ⲛ̀ⲕⲁⲑⲉⲕⲏⲥⲓⲥ ⲇ̄ ⲇⲉ ⲁϥ̀ⲓⲣⲓ· ⲟⲩⲓ̀ⲛϩⲁⲛⲁⲧⲟⲟⲩⲓ̀· ⲕⲉ ⲟⲩⲓ̀ ⲛ̀ϩⲁⲛⲁⲣⲟⲩϩ	في كل يوم، عملوا عظتين، واحدة باكراً، والاخرى للمساء	In a day, he made two homilies, one for the morning and another one for the evening.

CHAPTER XIII

TEXTUAL STRUCTURE OF THE RITE OF THE HOLY WEEK

We believe that the textual structure of Rite of the Holy Week is meshed like fabric, with horizontal and vertical integrations between the hours. We will explain this using the sext and none of Good Friday according to the earliest Manuscript of the Lectionary.

Rite	Sext	None	Remarks
1st reading	Nu 21:1-9 Bronze Serpent		Notice that the first and the last lesson of Sext deal with the exceptional events of this hour. The bolded text shows that the second and third lessons are complementary readings
2nd reading	Is 53:7-10 he was led like a sheep to the slaughter	Jer 11:18, 12:13 I had been like a sheep led obedient to the slaughter	
3rd reading	Is 12:2,13:1-10 And so you shall draw water with joy from the springs of deliverance	Zec 14:5-11. On that day living water shall issue from Jerusalem, half flowing to the eastern sea and...	

4th reading	Amos 8:9-12. I will make the sun go down at noon...		
1st Hymn	ⲑⲱⲕ ⲧⲉ ϯϫⲟⲙ → ⲧⲁⲓϣⲟⲩⲣⲏ ⲛⲛⲟⲩⲃ This golden and pure censer bearing the aroma is in the hands of Aaron the priest, who offers up incense on the altar	ⲑⲱⲕ ⲧⲉ ϯϫⲟⲙ → ϯϣⲟⲩⲣⲏ ⲛⲛⲟⲩⲃ The golden censer is the Virgin, her aroma is our Saviour. She gave birth to Him, He saved us and forgave our sins.	We may notice that the prayers of the sixth and ninth hours could complete each other either by reading the corresponding hymn in the none or the following hymn in the same hour
2nd Hymn	ⲫⲁⲓ ⲉⲧⲁϥⲉⲛϥ → This who offered himself upon the Cross as an acceptable sacrifice for the salvation of our race His Good Father smelled him on Golgotha in the evening	ⲫⲁⲓ ⲉⲧⲁϥⲉⲛϥ This who offered himself upon the Cross as an acceptable sacrifice for the salvation of our race His Good Father smelled him on Golgotha in the evening	It is important to mention that while the deacons are chanting this hymn, the priests offer the incense. Here we can see the harmony between the text, tunes and the actions.

Pauline Epistle	Gal 6:14-16. But God forbid that I should glory except in the Cross of our Lord Jesus Christ	Philipians 2:5-11. He humbled Himself and became obedient to the point of death even the death of the Cross. Therefore, God also has highly exalted Him.	
Troparia	O Thou Who on the 6th day, at the 6th hour, was nailed to the Cross, because of the sin which Adam dared (to commit) in the Paradise, tear up the handwriting of our sins, O Christ our God, and deliver us..."	"O Thou Who didst taste death in the flesh about the 9th hour on our account, slay our carnal thoughts, O Christ our God and deliver us."	

Troparia-	O only-begotten Son, the eternal and immortal Word of God; who for our salvation did will to be incarnate of the holy Theotokos and ever Virgin Mary, Who without changing becoming man and was crucified, the Christ God. Tramping down death by death. One of the Holy Trinity, who is glorified with the Father and the Holy Spirit, **_save_** us.		Especially for the sext
Trisagion	As usual	As usual	
Psalm/ Gospel			
Litany/ conclusion	As usual	As usual	
Faithfulness of the thief	Confession of the Thief		Especially for the sext

CONCLUSION

The book shows that the rite of the Holy Week in the Coptic Church descends from the rite of Jerusalem which was described by Egeria in 384 and the Armenian Lectionary of Jerusalem in the early fifth century..

Hymns were added to satisfy theological needs such as the troparion "Only Begotten"

Some hymns are added to explain the Gospel such as the hymn of "He who offered himself…"

In addition, there was some contribution to the hymns by our Syriac sister Church.

Despite the assumption that some think that the Lectionary of the Holy Week was arranged in the thirteenth century by the patriarch Gabriel Ibn Turaik, our study demonstrates that the original form reflects the rite of Jerusalem Coptic.

BIBLIOGRAPHY

القمص بطرس البرموسي، دراسة ونشر مخطوط مجموع قوانين لفرج الله الاخميمي المدون سنة 1357م دراسة الاصوام نموذجا، كلية الاداب جامعة الاسكندرية 2022

القمص عطالله ارسانيوس المحرقي. كتاب طروحات البصخة المقدسة. القاهرة 1969.

القمص عطالله ارسانيوس المحرقي. كتاب دلال اسبوع الالام المشتمل على ترتسب أسبوع الالام من يوم سبت لعازر الى يوم شم النسيم. القاهره 1970

القمص عطالله ارسانيوس. كتاب اللقان والسجده. القاهره 1971

ماجد صبحي رزق، شخصيات من تاريخنا (5) الانبا ميخائيل المعاريجي والقمص جرجس الحكيم""" الكرمة الجديدة 5 (2008) ص193-212

القمص فيلوثاوس المقاري و المعلم ميخائيل جرجس: كتاب طروحات البصخة المقدسة. الطبعه الاولي القاهرة 1914.

سمير خليل اليسوعي مصباح الظلمة في إيضاح الخدمة، /كتبة الكاروز 1971

صموئيل السرياني، تاريخ الكنائس والأديرة في القرن الثاني عشر لابو المكارم جرجس سعد الله والمنسوب خطاء لابي صالح الارمني، القاهرة 1984. 4 اجزاء

مطرانية بني سويف، دورة عيدي الصليب و الشعانين و طروحات البصخة المقدسة والخمسين حسب ترتيب الكنيسة القبطية الآرثوذكسية القاهرة 1983

ⲠⲒⲬⲰⲘ ⲚⲦⲈ ⲠⲒϪⲀⲒ ⲚⲦⲈ ⲠⲒⲤⲦⲀⲨⲢⲞⲤ ⲚⲈⲘ ⲪⲀ ⲠⲒϪⲀⲒ ⲚⲦⲈ ⲚⲒⲂⲀⲒ ⲚⲈⲘ ⲚⲒⲮⲀⲖⲒⲀ ⲚⲦⲈ ⲠⲒϨⲘⲈ ⲈⲐⲞⲨ ⲚⲈⲘ ⲚⲀ ⲚⲒ ⲠⲒ Ⲛ̄ ⲚⲈϨⲞⲞⲨ ⲈⲐⲞⲨ ⲔⲀⲦⲀ ϮⲈⲔⲔⲖⲎⲤⲒⲀ ⲈⲐⲞⲨ Ⲛ̄ⲢⲈⲘⲚ̄ⲬⲎⲘⲒ ⲚⲞⲢⲐⲞⲆⲞⲜⲞⲤ

R. TUKHI, ⲠⲒⲬⲰⲘ ⲚⲦⲈ ⲠⲒϢⲞⲘⲦ Ⲛ̄ⲀⲚⲀⲪⲞⲢⲀ ⲈⲦⲈ ⲚⲀⲒ ⲚⲈ ⲘⲠⲒⲀⲄⲒⲞⲤ ⲂⲀⲤⲒⲖⲒⲞⲤ ⲚⲈⲘ ⲠⲒⲀⲄⲒⲞⲤ ⲄⲢⲎⲄⲞⲢⲒⲞⲤ ⲠⲒⲐⲈⲞⲖⲞⲄⲞⲤ ⲚⲈⲘ ⲠⲒⲀⲄⲒⲞⲤ ⲔⲨⲢⲒⲖⲖⲞⲤ ⲚⲈⲘ ⲚⲒⲔⲈⲈⲨⲬⲎ ⲈⲐⲞⲨⲀⲂ, [the book of the three anaphoras which are that of saint Basil and saint Gregory the Theologian and saint Cyril and other holy prayers] Rome 1736.

Pauline ALLEN and Cornelia. DATEMA, *Leontius presbyter of Constantinople, Byzantina Australiensia* 9, Brisbane 1991.

B. ALTANER, *Patrology*, Eng. trans. Hilda Graef. London, 1958

Daliana ATANASSOVA, "Zu den Sahidischen Pascha-Lektionaren," *Coptic Studies on the threshold of a new Millenium, Proceeding of the International Congress of Coptic Studies Leiden 2000*, M. Immerzeel and J. Van der Vliet (eds)., Orientlia Lovansiansa Analecta 133, Vol.1, Leuven- Paris- Dudley 2004, p.607-620.

Aziz S. ATIYA; « Ibn Siba', Yuhanna Ibn Abi Zakariyya" in *Coptic Encyclopedia* 4, A.S. Atiya (ed.) New York: McMillan, 1991, pp.1272a-1272b.

Aziz S. ATIYA; "Ibn Kabar " in *Coptic Encyclopedia* 4, A.S. Atiya (ed.) New York: McMillan, 1991, pp.1267-1268.

J.H. BARKHUIZEN, "Justinian's Hymn O monogenh" uio" tou Qeou" *Byzantinische Zeitschrift* 77, (1984) 3-5.

Anton BAUMSTARK, «Drei greichische Passionsgesänge ägyptischer Liturgie» *Oriens Christianus* 3, (1929) 76.

Anton BAUMSTARK & W. HEFFENING, "Zwei altertümliche Litaneien aus dem Pashabuch der koptischen Kirche" *Oriens Christianus* 36 (1941) 74-100.

Anton BAUMSTARK, *Comparative Liturgy* - revised by Bernard BOTTE, English edition by F.L. Cross, London 1958.

Paul F. BRADSHAW, *The Search for the origins of Christian Workship – sources and Methods for the study of Early Liturgy*, Society for publication of Christian Knowledge (SPCK), London: University Press Cambridge 1992.

Maurice BRIÈRE, *Les Homiliae cathedrales de Sévère d'Antioche: Homélies CXX à CXXV.* Translated by Maurice Brière. Patrologia Orientalis 138 (29.1). Paris: Firmin-Didot, 1960.

Maurice BRIÈRE & François GRAFFIN, *Les Homiliae Cathedrales de Sévère d'Antioche*, Patrologia Orientalis 38 fasc.2 N° 175, Turnhout : Brepols 1976.

BIBLIOGRAPHY

F.E. BRIGHTMAN, *Liturgies Eastern and Western,* Oxford: Clarendon Press 1896.

Oswald Hugh Ewart BURMESTER, "The Canons of Christodulos, Patriarch of Alexandria, (A.D. 1047-1077)" *Le Muséon* 45, (1932) 71-84.

Oswald Hugh Ewart BURMESTER, "The Homilies or Exhortations of the Holy Week Lectionary." *Le Muséon* 45 (1932):21-70.

Oswald Hugh Ewart BURMESTER, *Le Lectionnaire de la Semaine Sainte,* Patrologia Orientalis 24 fasc.2 N° 117, Paris : Firmin-Didot 1933, p169-294.

Oswald Hugh Ewart BURMESTER "Two Services of the Coptic Church attributed to Peter, Bishop of Behnesa" *Le Muséon* 45 (1937) 235-254.

Oswald Hugh Ewart BURMESTER "Tûrûhat of the Coptic Church" *Orientlia Christiana Periodica* 3, (1937) 78-109.

Oswald Hugh Ewart BURMESTER, "Tûrûhat of the Coptic Year" *Orientalia Christiana Periodica* 3 (1937) 505-549.

Oswald Hugh Ewart BURMESTER *Le Lectionnaire de la Semaine Sainte,* Patrologia Orientalis 25, Fasc. 2 N° 122, Paris 1939, 175-485.

Oswald Hugh Ewart BURMESTER , *The rite of Consecration of the Patriarch of Alexandria,* Textes et documents, Le Caire: Socété d'Archéologie Copte 1960.

Oswald Hugh Ewart BURMESTER , *The Holrologion of the Egyptian Church,* Studia Orientalia Christiana Aegyptiaca, Cairo: Franciscan Center for Oriental Studies 1973.

Oswald Hugh Ewart BURMESTER , *Koptische Handschriften 2,* Verzeichnis der Orientalischen Handschriften in Deutschland, Band XXI/1, Wiesbaden: Franz Steiner Verlag 1975.

Alfred Joshua BUTLER see Basil Thomas EVETTS

Oswald Hugh Ewart BURMESTER R see Antoine KHATER

Charalambia COQUIN, *Les édifices Chrétiens du Vieux-Caire, volume 1, Bibliographie et topographie historiques,* Bibliothèque d'Études Coptes 11, Le Caire : Institut Français d'Archéologie Orientale 1974.

René Georges COQUIN, "Le Calendrier Copte des fêtes de saint chez al-Qalqashandi" *Mélanges à Eugène Tisserant, Parole de l'Orient* 6-7 (1975) 387-411.

René Georges COQUIN , «Langues et littérature Coptes» *Christianismes Orientaux*, Paris : CNRS-Cerf 1989.

René Georges COQUIN , «Ibn Kabar (Shams ar-Ri'asa Abû 'l-Barakat)» *Catholicisme* 6, 1966 col.1349-1351.

Jean CORBON, «Pourquoi les processions et autres pratiques rituelles?» *Proche Orient Chrétien* 46, (1996) 341-359.

Maria CRAMER, Studien zu koptischen Pascha-Büchern, Der Ritus des Karwoche in der Koptischen Kirche," *Oriens Christianus* 47 (1963) 118-128, 49 (1965) 90-115, 50 (1966) 72-130.

Walter Ewing CRUM, *Catalogue of the Coptic Manuscripts in the Collection of the John Rylands Library Manchester*, Manchester 1909.

Walter Ewing CRUM & A. EHRHARD, *Der Papyruscodex saec, vi-vii Phillips-bibliothek in Cheltenam* Schriften der Wissenschaftliche Gesellschaft in Strassburg 18 Heft, Strassburg: Karl J. Trübner 1915.

Walter Ewing CRUM & Hugh G. EVELYN-WHITE, The Monastery of Epiphanius at Thebes, Metropolitan Museum of Art, Egyptian Expedition, Part II, Coptic and Greek Ostraca and papyri, New York, 1926.

Walter Ewing CRUM see Wilhem RIEDEL.

Cornelia DATEMA see Pauline ALLEN.

Stephen DAVIS, Daniel SCHRIEVER and Mary FARAG, with the contribution of Samuel MOAWAD, *The feast of the desertt of Apa Shenoute, - A liturgical procession from the White Monastery in Upper Egypt*, Corpus Scriptorum Christianorum Orientalium 681 Coptici 53, Leuven: Peeters 2020.

Johannes DEN HEIJER, "The Composition of the History of the Churches and Monasteries of Egypt -Some preliminary remarks "*Acts of the Fifth International Congress of Coptic Studies Washington 12-15 August 1992,* ed D. Johnson, Vol 2 Part 1, Roma 1993, p 209-219.

Anna. DI BITONTO KASSER, "Due nuovi testi cristiani" *Aegyptus*, 79 (1999) 93-106.

BIBLIOGRAPHY

A. G, DRAGO, "Seeing Christ through Scriptures at the Paschal celebration: Exegesis as Mystery performance in the Paschal writing of Melito, Pseudo-Hippolytus and Origen," *Orientalia Chrsitiana Periodica* 74 (2008) 27-47.

Lucien DUCHESNE, *Early History of the Christian Church,* London 1924.

A. EHRHARD see Walter Ewing CRUM

Hugh G. EVELYN-WHITE see Walter Ewing CRUM.

Basil Thomas EVETTS and Alfred Joshua BUTLER, *The Churches and Monasteries of Egypt and some Neighbouring countries, attributed to Abû Salih the Armenian,* Oxford: Clarendon press 1895.

Mary FARAG, see Stephen DAVIS, Daniel SCHRIEVER and with the contribution of Samuel MOAWAD

J. M FIEY, "Coptes et Syriaques, Contacts et Echanges" *Studia Orientalia Chistiana Collectanae* 15 (1972-1973), 295-366.

W. H. C. FREND, *The Rise of the Monophysite Movement,* 2nd ed., Cambridge: Cambridge University press 1979.

Maurice GEERARD, *Clavis Patrum Graecorum,* Volume 3. Corpus Christianorum Turnhout: Brepols 1978.

Maurice GEERARD, *Clavis Patrum Graecorum, Patres Antenicaeni,* Corpus Christianorum, Volume 1, Turnhout: Brepols 1983.

Georg GRAF, *Verzeichnis arabischen kirchlichen Termini,* Corpus Scriptorum Christianorum Orientalium 147, Louvain 1954.

François GRAFFIN see Maurice BRIÈRE.

Bishop GREGORIUS, "Feast, Minor" in *Coptic Encyclopedia* 4, A.S. Atiya (ed.) New York: McMillan, 1991, p. p. 1106a-1109b.

Robert GRIVEAU, *Les fêtes Coptes par Maqrizi par al-Maqrizi -* Patrologia Orientalis 10 fasc.4 No 49, Paris : Firmin-Didot 1915, p.287-356.

Victor GRUMEL, «L'auteur et la date de composition du tropaire o monogenh»» *Echos d'Orient* 22, (1923) 398-418.

Antoine GUILLAUMONT, *Aux origines du monachisme chrétien,* Spiritualité Orientale N°30, Bellefontaine 1979, p168-183.

W. HEFFENING see Anton BAUMSTARK.

E. JEFFREYS, M. JEFFREYS, Roger SCOTT, *The Chronicle of John Malalas,* Byzantina Australiensa 4, Melbourne 1986.

Rodolphe KASSER, «La 'Prière de Jésus' kelliote» *Orientalia Christiana Periodica* 62, (1996) 407-410.

Antoine KHATER and Oswald Hugh Ewart BURMESTER, *Catalogue of the Coptic and Christian Arabic Mss preserved in the Cloister of Saint Menas at Cairo, Bibliothèque de Manuscrits* I, Le Caire: Société d'Archéologie Copte 1967.

Antoine KHATER and Oswald Hugh Ewart BURMESTER, , *History of the Patriarchs of the Egyptian Church, Vol III part I-* Textes et Documents XI, Le Caire: Société d'Archéologie Copte 1968.

Antoine KHATER and Oswald Hugh Ewart BURMESTER, *Catalogue of the Coptic and Christian Arabic Mss preserved in the Library of the Church of the all-Holy Virgin Mary known as Qasrîat ar-Rihân at Old Cairo, Bibliothèque de Manuscrits* II, Le Caire: Le Caire:Société d'Archéologie Copte 1973.

A. KING, *The Rites of Eastern Christendom.* Città del Vaticano 1948, Vol I.

André LOSSKY, "Le mot aujourd'hui " dans les hymnes Byzantines de fêtes : une actualisation de l'événement célébré » in *Rites de communion, conférences Saint-Serge. LVIe Semaine d'études liturgiques,* A. Lossky et M. Sodi (eds) Città del Vaticano 2011, p.283-295.

L. S. B. MACCOULL, "Stud. Pal. XV 250 ab: a Monophysite Trishagion for the Nile Flood" *Journal of Theological Studies* 40, (1989) 129-135.

Hanna MALAK, «Les Livres liturgiques de l'Église Copte» *Mélanges Eugène Tisserant, Studi e Testi* 233, Vatican 1964, p1-35.

Pierre MARAVAL, Egérie, *Journal de Voyage (Itinéraire) et Lettre sur la Bienheureuse. Egérie,* Sources Chrétiennes 296, Textes et traduction, Paris :Cerf 1982

Maurice MARTIN, SJ, «Le Delta chrétien à la fin du XII° s» *Orientalia Christiana Periodica* 63 (1997) 181-199.

Maurice MARTIN , SJ, «Alexandrie chrétienne à la fin du XII° d'après Abû l-Makârim» *Alexandrie médiévale 1*, Christian. DÉCOBERT et Jean Yves EMPEREUR (eds), Études alexandrines 3, Cairo 1998, p 45-49.

Maurice MARTIN SJ, «Chrétiens et musulmans à la fin du XII° siècle» *Valeur et distance: Identités et Sociétés en Égypte*, Paris 2000, p.83-92.

Maurice MARTIN , SJ, «Dévotions populaires au Caire à la fin du XIIᵉ siècle» *Aegyptus Christiana, Mélanges d'Hagiographie Égyptienne et Orientale dédiés à la mémoire du P. Paul Devos* Bollandiste, Ugo ZANETTI et Enzo LUCCHESI (eds), (coll. « Cahiers d'Orientalisme XXV », Genève 2004, p.313-320.

Jean MASPERO, *Histoire des Patriarches d'Alexandrie 518-616, Bibliothèque de l'école Pratiques des Hautes Études* 237, Paris 1923.

John MEYENDORFF, *Christ in Eastern Christian Thought*, St. Vladimir's Seminary Press 1975.

Vincentio MISTRIH, *Pretiosa Margarita de Scientiis Ecclesiasticis*, Juhanna Ibn Abi Zakaria Ibn Siba', Studia Orientalia Christiana Aegyptiaca, Cairi 1966.

Samuel MOAWADsee Stephen DAVIS, Daniel SCHRIEVER and Mary FARAG.

Ragheb MOFTAH, Marian ROBERTSON, Martha ROY, Margit TOTH, "Music. Coptic" in *Coptic Encyclopedia* 6, A.S. Atiya (ed.) New York: McMillan, 1991, p. **1715a-1747b**.

Ray MOUAWAD, "Un parallèle intéressant à propos du Trisagion entre le "Muršid" de Yahya ibn Garir (XIe S.) et le "Livre des 10 chapitres" de Thomas Kfartab (XIe s.)" *Parole de l'Orient* 28 (2003), 537-550.

Guido MÜLLER, *Lexicon Athanasium,* Berlin: Walter De Gruyter 1952.

Jacob MUYSER, «Le Psali copte pour la première heure du samedi de la joie» *Le Muséon* 61, (1952), 175-184.

François NAU, *Un Martyrologe et douze Ménologes Syriaques,* Patrologia Orientalis 10 fasc. 1 Number 46, Paris : Firmin-Didot 1912.

Tito ORLANDI, "Due fogli papiracei da Medinet Madi (Fayum): l'historia Horsiesi" *Egitto e Vicino Oriente* 13 (1990) 109-126.

Malcolm PEEL, "Dayr Epiphanius" in *Coptic Encyclopedia,* A.S. Atiya (ed.) Volume 2, New York: MacMillan 1991, p.800b- 802b.

Johannes QUASTEN, *Patrology, the beginnings of the Patristic Literature,* volume 1, Utrecht-Antwerp: Spectrums Publishers 1966.

Johannes QUASTEN, *Initiation aux Pères de l'Église,* Vol III, Paris : Cerf 1987.

Athanase RENOUX, *Le Codex Arménien Jérusalem 121, I Introduction aux origines de la liturgies Hiérosolymitaine lumières nouvelles,* Patrologia Orientalis 35, fasc. 1 No 163, Turnhout : Brepols 1969, pp. 1-215.

Athanase RENOUX, *Le Codex Arménien Jérusalem 121, II Éditions comparée du Texte et deux autres manuscrits, introduction, textes, traduction et notes.* Patrologia Orientalis 36, fasc. 2 No 168, Turnhout : Brepols 1971, pp144-289.

Charles RENOUX, "les chants de communion de l'hymnaire de Saint-Sabas" in *Rites de communion, conférences Saint-Serge. LVe Semaine d'études liturgiques,* A. Lossky et M. Sodi (eds) Città del Vaticano 2010, pp.81-91.

.Wilhem RIEDEL and Walter Ewing CRUM, *The Canons of Athanasius of Alexandria*, Text and Translation Society, London: Williams and Norgate 1904.

Marian ROBERTSON "A Coptic Melody Sung Interchangeably in Different Languages: Comparisons thereof and Proposed Dating therefore" *Coptic Studies Acts of the Third International Congress of Coptic Studies,* Varsovie 1990, p365-371.

Marian ROBERTSON, see Ragheb MOFTAH, Martha ROY, Margit TOTH.

Martha ROY, see Ragheb MOFTAH, Marian ROBERTSON, Margit TOTH.

SAMIR KHALIL, «Un manuscrit arabe d'Alep reconnu, le Sbath 1125» *Le Muséon* 91, (1978) 179-188.

SAMIR KHALIL, "L'encyclopedie Liturgique d'Ibn Kabar (+ 1324) et son apologie d'usage Coptes" *Crossword of Cultures Studies in Liturgy and patristics in Honor of Gabriele Winkler,* edited by H.-J. FEULNER, E. VELKOUSKA and R. TAFT, *Orientalia Christiana Analecta* 260, Roma 2000, p. 629-655.

SAMUEL AL-SURIANI, «Icônes et iconographie d'après le manuscrit d'Abu el-Makarim, publié en arabe au Caire 1984» *Le Monde Copte* 18, (1990) 78.

Daniel SCHRIEVER see Stephen DAVIS, and Mary FARAG, with the contribution of Samuel MOAWAD.

Eric SEGELBERG, "Hippolytus" *Coptic Encyclopedia,* A. S. Atiya (ed.) volume 4, New York: MacMillan 1991, p. 1235-1236.

Roger SCOTT see E. JEFFREYS, M. JEFFREYS.

Adel SIDARUS, «La pâque Sainte ou La Semaine Sainte selon la liturgie Copte,» *Proche Orient Chrétien* 17, (1967) 1-43.

Adel SIDARUS, «La Semaine Sainte à Daîr as-Suriân,» *Bulletin de la Société d'Archéologie Copte* 20, (1969-1970) 5-32.

Marcus SIMAIKA and Yassa 'ABD AL-MASIH, *Catalogue of the Coptic and Arabic Manuscripts in the Coptic Museum, the Patriarchate, the Principal Churches of Cairo and Alexandria and the Monasteries of Egypt,* Vol II Fasc. I, Cairo: Coptic Museum 1942.

Ernest STEIN, *Histoire du Bas-Empire*, Tome premier, Paris 1959.

Lothar STÖRK, *Koptische Handschriften 2,* Verzeichnis der Orientalischen Handschriften in Deutschland, Band XXI/2, Stuttgart: Franz Steiner Verlag, 1995.

Robert TAFT, *The Great Entrance,* Orientalia Christiana Analecta 200, Roma: Pontificio Istituto Orientale 1978.

Michel TARCHNISCHVILI, *Le Grand lectionnaire de l'Église de Jérusalem (V*- *VIII*^{e} *siècle)* Corpus Scriptorum Christianorum Orientalium 189 Scriptores Iberici 10, Louvain 1959.

Janet TIMBIE, « Once more into the desert of Shenoute, further thoughts on BN68 » *Christianity and Monasticism in Upper Egypt,* Gawdat GABRA and Hany N. TAKLA (eds) Volume 1, A Saint Mark Foundation, the American University in Cairo Press, Cairo- New York 2008, pp169-178.

Margit TOTH, see Ragheb MOFTAH, Marian ROBERTSON, Martha ROY.

Gérard TROUPEAU, *Catalogue des Manuscrits Arabes -première partie Manuscrits Chrétiens,* Paris: Bibliothèque Nationale de Paris 1974.

Armand VEILLEUX, *Pachomian Koinonia,* Cistercian Studies Series 45-47, Michigan 1980-1982.

Louis VILLECOURT, *Le livre de la lampe des Ténèbres et de l'exposition (lumineuse) du service (de l'Église) par Abû 'l-Barakât connu sous le nom d'Ibn Kabar, Chapitre I-II* Patrologia Orientalis 20 fasc. 4, No 99, Paris : Firmin Didot 1928, p. 575-734.

Louis VILLECOURT,, «Les observances liturgiques et la discipline du Jeûne dans l'Église Copte» *Le Muséon* 36 (1922) 249-292 ; 37 (1924) 201-280 ; 38 (1925) 261-320.

A. WADI, "Abu al-Barakat Ibn Kabar, Misbah al-Zulmah (cap. 18: il digiuno e la settimanta santa" *Studia Orientalia Christiana Collectanea* 34 (2001), 233-322

John WILKINSON, *Egeria's Travel,* Warminster: Aris & Philips Ltd, 1999.

Wolfgang WITAKOWSWKI, *Pseudo-Dionysius of Tel-Mahre, Chronicle Part III,* translated with notes, Translated Texts for Historians 22, Liverpool: Liverpool University Press 1996.

Youhanna Nessim YOUSSEF, «Une relecture des Théotokies Coptes» *Bulletin de la Société d'Archéologie Copte* 36 (1997) 157-170.

Youhanna Nessim YOUSSEF, "Multiconfessional churches in Egypt during the XII Century," *Bulletin of Saint Shenouda the Archmandrite Coptic Society* 5 (1998-1999) 45-54.

Youhanna Nessim YOUSSEF, "Notes on the traditions concerning the Trisagion" *Parole de l'Orient* 29 (2004) 147-159.

Youhanna Nessim YOUSSEF, « Les textes en dialecte sahidique: du MS 106 Lit., Bibliothèque Patriarcale-au Caire (La coction myron)» *Bulletin de la Société d'Archéologie Copte* 37, (1998) 121-134.

Youhanna Nessim YOUSSEF, "Consecration of the Myron at Saint Macarius Monastery (MS. 106Lit.)" *Coptica* 2 (2003), 106-121.

"Consecration of the Myron at Saint Macarius Monastery (Ms 106 Lit.) *Christianity and Monasticism in Egypt*, Maged S.A. MIKHAIL and Mark MOUSSA (eds) A Saint Mark Foundation, the American University in Cairo Press, Cairo- New York 2009, p. 106-121.

Youhanna Nessim YOUSSEF , " La doxologie des êtres célestes et son importance liturgique, " in A. BOUD'HORS et C. LOUIS (éds) *Études Coptes XIII, Quinzième journée d'études (Louvain-La Neuve, 12-*

14 mai 2011), Cahiers de la Bibliothèque Copte 20, Paris : de Boccard 2015, pp. 295-305.

Youhanna Nessim YOUSSEF, "Psali of the Lectionary (revisited) Yûsif the hymnographer," *Bulletin de la Société d'Archéologie Copte* 55 (2016) 143-174.

Youhanna Nessim YOUSSEF and Ugo ZANETTI, *La consécration du Myron par Gabriel IV, 86ᵉ patriarche d'Alexandrie en 1374,* Jerusalemer Theologisches Forum 20, Münster: Aschendorff Verlag 2014.

Ugo ZANETTI, «Esquisse d'une typologie des euchologes coptes bohaïriques» *Le Muséon* 100, (1987) 407-418.

Ugo ZANETTI, « Is the Ethiopian Holy Week Service translated from Sahidic? Towards a study of the Gebra Hemâmât." In *Proceeding of the Eleventh International Conference of the Ethiopian Studies, Addis Ababa, 1-6 April 1991,* B. ZEWDE, R. PANKHUST and T. BEYENE (eds.), vol. 1, Addis Ababa: Institute of Ethiopian Studies 1994, pp. 450-462.

Ugo ZANETTI, «Abu L-Makarim et Abu Salih» *Bulletin de la Société d'Archéologie Copte* 34 (1995) 85-133.

Ugo ZANETTI, « Liturgy at Wadi al-Natrun," *Coptica* 2 (2003)122-141.

Ugo ZANETTI,see Youhanna Nessim YOUSSEF

Website

The English text is taken from the translation prepared by John Abela ofm based on articles and research by Virgilio Corbo ofm, Michele Piccirillo ofm and Eugenio Alliata ofm http://www.christusrex.org/www1/jhs/TSeger04.html#Target15

W. Christ-M. Paranikas, "*Anthologia Graeca carminum Christianorum,* Lipsieae 1971, p52,

Georgius Monachos, *Chronicon* C de Boor, *Bibliotheca Scriptorum Graecorum et Romanorum Teubneriana,* Leipzig 1904 , ²ed Wirth Stuttgart1978, Vol II, p627.3.7

APPENDIX

http://www.ccel.wheaton.edu/fathers2/NPNF2-05/Npnf2-05-33.htm#P2974_2009392

On Pilgrimages1

Since, my friend, you ask me a question in your letter, I think that it is incumbent upon me to answer you in their proper order upon all the points connected with it. It is, then, my opinion that it is a good thing for those who have dedicated themselves once for all to the higher life to fix their attention continually upon the utterances in the Gospel, and, just as those who correct their work in any given material by a rule, and by means of the straightness of that rule bring the crookedness which their hands detect to straightness, so it is right that we should apply to these questions a strict and flawless measure as it were,-I mean, of course, the Gospel rule of life2,-and in accordance with that, direct ourselves in the sight of God. Now there are some amongst those who have entered upon the monastic and hermit life, who have made it a part of their devotion to behold those spots at Jerusalem where the memorials of our Lord's life in the flesh are on view; it would be well, then, to look to this Rule, and if the finger of its precepts points to the observance of such things, to perform the work, as the actual injunction of our Lord; but if they lie quite outside the commandment of the Master, I do not see what there is to command any one who has become a law of duty to himself to be zealous in performing any of them. When the Lord invites the blest to their inheritance in the kingdom of heaven, He does not include a pilgrimage to Jerusalem amongst their good deeds; when He announces the Beatitudes, He does not name amongst them that sort of devotion. But as to that which neither makes us blessed nor sets us in the path to the kingdom, for what reason it should be run after, let him that is wise consider. Even if there were some profit in what they do, yet even so, those who are perfect would do best not to be eager in practicing it; but since this matter, when closely looked into, is found to inflict upon those who have begun to lead the stricter life a moral mischief, it is so far from being worth an earnest pursuit, that it actually requires the greatest caution to prevent him who has devoted himself to God from being penetrated by any of its hurtful influences. What is it, then, that is hurtful in it? The Holy Life is open to all, men and women alike. Of that contemplative Life the peculiar mark is Modesty3 . But Modesty is preserved in societies that live distinct and separate, so that there should be no meeting and mixing up of persons of opposite sex; men are not to rush to keep the rules of Modesty in the company of women, nor women to do so in the company of men. But the necessities of a journey are continually apt to reduce this scrupulousness to a very indifferent observance of such rules. For instance, it is impossible for a woman to accomplish so long a journey without a conductor; on account of her natural weakness she has to be put upon her horse and to be lifted down again; she has to be supported4 in difficult situations. Whichever we suppose, that she has an acquaintance to do this yeoman's service, or a hired attendant to perform it, either way the proceeding cannot escape being reprehensible; whether she leans on the help of a stranger, or on that of her own servant, she fails to keep the law of correct conduct; and as the inns and hostelries and cities of the East present many examples of licence and of indifference to vice, how will it be possible for one passing through such smoke to escape without smarting eyes? Where the ear and the eye is defiled, and the heart too, by receiving all those foulnesses through eye and ear, how will it be possible to thread without infection such seats of contagion? What advantage, moreover, is reaped by him who reaches those celebrated spots themselves? He cannot imagine that our Lord is living, in the body, there at the present day, but has gone away from us foreigners; or that the Holy Spirit is in abundance at Jerusalem, but unable to travel as far as us. Whereas, if it is really possible to infer God's presence from visible symbols, one might more justly consider that He dwelt in the Cappadocian nation than in any of the spots outside it. For how many Altars5 there are there, on which the name of our Lord is glorified! One could hardly count so many in all the rest of the world. Again, if the Divine grace was more abundant about Jerusalem than elsewhere, sin would not be so much the fashion amongst those that live there; but as it is, there is no form of uncleanness6 that is not perpetrated amongst them; rascality, adultery, theft, idolatry, poisoning, quarrelling, murder, are rife; and the last kind of evil is so excessively prevalent, that nowhere in the world are people so ready to kill each other as there; where kinsmen attack each other like wild beasts, and spill each other's blood, merely for the sake of lifeless plunder. Well, in a place where such things go on, what proof, I ask, have you of the abundance of Divine grace? But I know what many will retort to all that I have said, they will say, "Why did you not lay down this rule for yourself as well? If there is no gain for the godly pilgrim in return for having been there, for what reason did you undergo the toil of so long a journey?" Let them hear from me my plea for this.

By the necessities of that office in which I have been placed by the Dispenser of my life to live, it was my duty, for the purpose of the correction which the Holy Council had resolved upon, to visit the places where the Church in Arabia is; secondly, as Arabia is on the confines of the Jerusalem district, I had promised that I would confer also with the Heads of the Holy Jerusalem Churches, because matters with them were in confusion, and needed an arbiter; thirdly, our most religious Emperor had granted us facilities for the journey, by postal conveyance, so that we had to endure none of those inconveniences which in the case of others we have noticed; our wagon was, in fact, as good as a church or monastery to us, for all of us were singing psalms and fasting in the Lord during the whole journey. Let our own case therefore cause difficulty to none; rather let our advice be all the more listened to, because we are giving it upon matters which came actually before our eyes. We confessed that the Christ Who was manifested is very God, as much before as after our sojourn at Jerusalem; our faith in Him was not increased afterwards any more than it was diminished. Before we saw Bethlehem, we knew His being made man by means of the Virgin; before we saw His Grave we believed in His Resurrection from the dead; apart from seeing the Mount of Olives, we confessed that His Ascension into heaven was real. We derived only thus much of profit from our travelling thither, namely that we came to know by being able to compare them, that our own places are far holier than those abroad. Wherefore, O ye who fear the Lord, praise Him in the places where ye now are. Change of place does not effect any drawing nearer unto God, but wherever thou mayest be, God will come to thee, if the chambers of thy soul be found of such a sort that He can dwell in thee and walk in thee. But if thou keepest thine inner man full of wicked thoughts, even if thou wast on Golgotha, even if thou wast on the Mount of Olives, even if thou stoodest on the memorial-rock of the Resurrection, thou wilt be as far away from receiving Christ into thyself, as one who has not even begun to confess Him. Therefore, my beloved friend, counsel the brethren to be absent from the body to go to our Lord, rather than to be absent from Cappadocia to go to Palestine; and if any one should adduce the command spoken by our Lord to His disciples that they should not quit Jerusalem, let him be made to understand its true meaning. Inasmuch as the gift and the distribution of the Holy Spirit had not yet passed upon the Apostles, our Lord commanded them to remain in the same place, until they should have been endued with power from on high. Now, if that which happened at the beginning, when the Holy Spirit was dispensing each of His gifts under the appearance of a flame, continued until now, it would be right for all to remain in that place where that dispensing took place; but if the Spirit "bloweth" where He "listeth," those, too, who have become believers here are made partakers of that gift; and that according to the proportion of their faith, not in consequence of their pilgrimage to Jerusalem.

Notes

1 The modern history of this Letter is curious. Its genuineness though suspected by Bellarmine, is admitted by Tillemont, and even by Caesar Baronius. After having been edited by Morel in Greek and Latin, 1551, it was omitted from his son's edition of the works of Gregory by the advice of Fronto Ducaeus, lest it should seem to reflect upon the practice of pilgrimages. But in 1607 it was again edited (Hannov.) by Du Moulin, with a defence of it, and a translation into French by R.

APPENDIX 133

Stephen: this is the only instance of a vernacular version of Gregory at this time, and shows the importance attached to this Letter. It appears in the second Paris Edition, but with the vehement protests, printed in the notes, of the Jesuit Gretser, against Du Moulin's interpretation of its scope, and even against its genuineness. He makes much of its absence from the Bavarian (Munich) Cod., and of the fact that even "heretical printers" had omitted it from the Basle Edition of 1562: and he is very angry with Du Moulin for not having approached the Royal Library while in Paris, and while he had leisure from his "Calvinistic evening communions." But why should he, when the Librarian, no less a person than I. Casaubon (appointed 1598), had assured him that the Letter was in the Codex Regius? It is in Migne iii. col.1009. See Letter to Eustathia, &c.

2 politeian, "vivendi rationem." Cf. Basil, Homil. xiii.

3 h eusxhmosunh.

4 parakratoumenh; cf. Epict. (cited by Diosc.) taj trixaj reousaj parakratein, "to stop the hair from falling off."

5 qusiasthria, the sanctuaries (with the Altar), into which at this time no layman except the Emperor might enter (Balsamon's note to decrees of Council of

Laodicaea).

6 Cyril's Catecheses in the year 348 had combated the practical immorality of the Holy City.

Manuscript of Uppsala of Ibn Kabar

ونجب السكون نصاب اتلله من ليوت ⊕ وتقول الشماس من لوتكت مصوت
السيد ⊕ وعند هيكل كاسا نفل الدلمس تنت ⊕ وبيت العمويد يقري
فصل من لوقا دامت مريم ⊕ والدى يعتمد يد الرهبان بدى شهران
انهم اولا ارى صورة وتقول عند هايقوم ونصلا لانقابها ⊕ واى موضع فلا
اليه من مواضع القدس قم وانه نصلا لدلالا هما ⊕ مالله عبد لهما كالفصول
التى يضى ذكر المشكل وبيت الاعوان مايليق وكان ليرم بها ⊕ وعند
الطاهر والعبيد فصل الخبر ⊕ عند المايد الادفه حتى الخيرات بسبع
الخبرات ⊕ عند البيت فصل السايم ⊕ عند الفم وفصل من سول
الامور الواردة كتاب التغير للواحد بماياه ⊕ واما التريب في دلالا سبا
لقد سريعا يوس فاند جارى على مار ويدعه دوار بهم الزيتون ليدخول الدير
وخلفة جاربه وا اهل الصعيد لهم الهومسيات والدعات المستبطم من
المزابر الذار ودية الدال عليها دلالا لهم السى بالكهون يسحجرون باكارة
ورادتبا تتيا طويلا حتى يا لما الكل كان يمرون به وكل شى يعبرون على
منع او رجل او حمار ابعشب او شجر او غير ذلك ⊕ ثم أن عادة السرين
بعد دور الثحية الى هيكل الصلاة ونصلى صلاة الاعيار وطرح المزمور ويقرى
فصل من الجل بكمل الصلاة ومقدم القداس ⊕ ولا نفد ولى ذكر ص بالقداس
لغبو يوس او ياسلوت رالاجب لغبو ومرك لحصاص بالاعياد السيدة
والافراح الالهية ⊕ واذا فرغ الدلاس تشرعوا المغرب لابتهال مزمور الله
ليصدر أصول التجبير فصلا بعد فصل من يبلاع على لسن الشار ابر والاجبل

www.ingramcontent.com/pod-product-compliance
Lightning Source LLC
Chambersburg PA
CBHW032301150426
43195CB00008BA/535